Employee Relations Explained

Employee Relations Explained

Gemma Dale

KoganPage

First published in Great Britain and the United States in 2025 by Kogan Page Limited

Kogan Page
Kogan Page Ltd, 2nd Floor, 45 Gee Street, London EC1V 3RS, United Kingdom
Kogan Page Inc, 8 W 38th Street, Suite 902, New York, NY 10018, USA
www.koganpage.com

EU Representative (GPSR)
Authorised Rep Compliance Ltd, Ground Floor, 71 Baggot Street Lower, Dublin D02 P593, Ireland
www.arccompliance.com

Kogan Page books are printed on paper from sustainable forests.

© Kogan Page, 2025

ISBNs
Hardback   978 1 3986 2445 0
Paperback   978 1 3986 2560 0
Ebook   978 1 3986 2447 4

British Library Cataloguing-in-Publication Data
A CIP record for this book is available from the British Library.

Typeset by Hong Kong FIVE Workshop, Hong Kong
Printed and bound by CPI Group (UK) Ltd, Croydon CR0 4YY

Contents

Introduction

Introducing this book

This book has been written with the early-career Human Resources (HR) professional in mind. You may be a recent HR graduate, undertaking your first role in HR, or be in the early stages of your HR career. This book may also interest people managers if they wish to learn more about employee relations and build their skills in handling common employee relations issues.

Depending on your current HR role, you may or may not be involved in delivering each of the different subjects discussed in this book. However, we have aimed to provide a comprehensive summary of each topic and how it is practically implemented in organizations to ensure that you have a full understanding of this interesting element of HR work.

Throughout the book, you will find a range of reflection points, tips and exercises. Each tip is based on recognized good practice for managing employee relations activities. Each chapter also has review questions to test your learning and understanding, as well as further reading suggestions. Use the endnotes to discover more about any research, reports or publications from other organizations discussed throughout.

The reflection points, review questions and exercises included throughout the chapters are designed to deepen your learning and set the subjects of individual and collective employee relations in your own unique organizational context. Not every exercise will necessarily be relevant to your current role and responsibilities; you should undertake the ones that you feel are most relevant to you and your role or the direction you wish to pursue in your future career.

Some reflection questions are called 'What would you do?'. These ask you to reflect on what you would do in specific scenarios. There are not necessarily any 'right' answers to these exercises – only ones that are informed by the context, detail and organizational policies. These answers are not a substitute for legal advice on specific circumstances. Sometimes, the answer will need you to assess employee relations risks. Think about what you would do in these scenarios, using the content in the chapter when necessary to determine your answer. If you are not currently in an HR role, you can reflect on any other work that you have done previously, or simply think about how you would approach the situation if it arose in a future HR role. After you have had a chance to reflect, you can then visit the Appendix, where you will find suggested answers.

Remember that the HR role is a broad one, and you should consider any tips and suggestions in the context of your own organizational culture. Depending on where you are based, there may also be local laws that relate to many of the subjects in this book, so before making any recommendations or taking action always check if there are any additional requirements you should consider first.

A brief introduction to employee relations

> **Employee relations:** A term used to describe the relationships between employees and their employers.

Employee relations is a broad term. Traditionally, it focused on the collective relationship between employers and employee representatives such as trade unions, and historically has sometimes been referred to as 'industrial relations' or 'labour relations'. We take a brief look at the history of employee relations in Chapter 2.

Today, employee relations can encompass many ideas and perspectives. Often, the work of employee relations sits within the work of HR; it may be a specialist team or function, or the activities may form part of the work of generalist HR professionals.

Employee relations includes collective relationships, encompassing organizational culture and how organizations can create positive working relationships with their employees. Here we can see similarities with the work of employee engagement and experience (often also part of the work of HR professionals) – terms we will explore fully throughout this book.

Employee relations also takes into account the tensions and difficulties that can arise in the employment relationship, either formally or informally, and how these are addressed and managed. In practice, employee relations is also about policy, procedure, and sometimes legal issues.

The structure of this book

Within this book, we consider the broader relationships between work and workers, and some of the important political and legal dimensions. We also discuss the kind of work that is often undertaken within the scope of employee relations, both collectively and individually. Early career HR professionals are often involved in the practical side of employee relations, including managing conflict or addressing underperformance, so this has a particular focus throughout many of the chapters.

In summary, this book addresses the following elements of employee relations from the perspective of the early career HR professional:

- The relationship between employees and employers and how this is managed by organizations, both individually and collectively.
- Employee relations in practice, including managing aspects of the employment relationship including performance, behaviour and conduct.

> **TIP**
>
> This book focuses predominantly on the UK legal system – although sometimes there can be differences in the law between England, Scotland, Wales and Northern Ireland. Readers should check their local or domestic legislation in addition to the content presented here.

In Chapter 1, we explore what we mean by employee relations in practice; what is good employee relations, and what happens when employee relations are poor? We also discuss the work included within employee relations and the skills needed to undertake it.

Chapter 2 focuses on collective employee relations, discussing employee participation, trade unions and consultation and negotiation. Chapter 3 looks at individual and collective conflict at work, and how employee relations work can help to manage and prevent it.

Chapters 4, 5 and 6 turn to individual aspects of the employment relationship. They focus on the practical application of employee relations, looking at how to manage performance, conduct and behaviour and absence respectively. Chapter 7 looks at some of the more complex, sensitive and difficult issues that can arise during employee relations. Chapter 8 returns to strategic considerations and discusses how organizations can work towards achieving good relations with their employees.

Finally, the Conclusion provides an opportunity for you to reflect on your current skills, behaviours and knowledge and create a plan for future learning and development.

CHAPTER ONE

Introducing employee relations

Introduction

Employee relations is a broad term, and it can mean different things to different people. It also has some similarities and links to other terms related to employment and the employee relationship. We therefore begin this chapter with a discussion about the term, defining some key concepts, and crucially examining how it interacts with employment law.

We then consider what we mean by good employee relations, and why it is so important that organizations manage the employment relationship. Finally, we consider employee relations from the perspective of the early career HR professional, reviewing the kinds of activities that might fall within your roles and responsibilities, comparing that to the role of people managers, and identifying the skills required to be effective within the field of employee relations.

LEARNING OBJECTIVES

By the end of this chapter, you will be able to:

- Define 'employee relations' and other related key terms and concepts.

- Describe how employment law affects employee relations work.
- Summarize the importance of good employee relations and how it can contribute to organizational outcomes.
- Define the role of HR professionals in practical employee relations and how it differs from that of people managers.
- Identify the HR skills and competencies necessary for effective employee relations and how these might be developed by early career professionals.
- Explain some of the common challenges you are likely to encounter in employee relations and how to overcome them.

Introducing employee relations

As we discussed in the Introduction to this book, employee relations is often part of the work of HR professionals. It is also the responsibility of leaders and managers, as the decisions they make can influence relations with employees. Managers also influence employee relations through their day-to-day work, not just their decision-making.

Employee relations refers to the relationship between employees and employers. This encompasses the collective relationship between workers and employers (often through employee representative groups such as trade unions). It also includes the relationship between employers and individual employees. Both of these form part of the work of HR professionals. We will begin by exploring some of these concepts and terms.

Employee relations concepts

Several concepts and terms relate to the broad field of employee relations. As you will see, employee relations is linked to and interconnected with other aspects of human resource management. Together, these different elements form part of the overarching relationships between employees, managers and the organization as a whole.

EMPLOYEE ENGAGEMENT

Employee engagement is generally considered to be a psychological state related to how employees feel about their work and the organization that they work for. Like many of the terms here, it has a broad meaning and is sometimes described as an 'umbrella' term that encompasses lots of different ideas about people at work. It is often associated with other ideas such as job satisfaction, motivation, commitment to work, effort, pride and enthusiasm, and employees who 'go the extra mile' or give discretionary effort to their work. Engagement can also include the extent to which employees identify with their work or the meaning they find in it. In recent years there has been considerable interest in employee engagement, and many organizations often undertake engagement surveys to learn more about how their employees feel about them and their work.

EMPLOYEE VOICE

Voice describes the ways that employees can provide feedback, contribute their perspectives and influence those things that affect their working lives. It includes informal and formal methods, such as employee engagement surveys, suggestions schemes or consultation with trade unions. Voice is a key aspect of employee relations; it is also a driver of employee engagement. We will explore employee voice in more depth in Chapter 8.

EMPLOYEE EXPERIENCE

Employee experience is a general term used to describe the total experience an employee has of working for a particular employer. It includes HR-type activities such as induction or training but is much broader than that, encompassing the systems that they use, the interactions that they have with people who work for the organization, the workplace itself and ways of working. A good overall experience is also related to employee engagement and employee relations. In recent years there has been an increase in interest in this idea, and some organizations now think about how to design for a good employee experience as well as aim to improve employee engagement.

PSYCHOLOGICAL CONTRACT

This term is used to describe the unwritten agreement between employees and employers, comprised of the employee's beliefs and expectations about their job and their work. A fairly nebulous idea, it includes expectations about how employees believe they will be treated, what the working relationship will be like in practice and what commitments are made to each other – but these are not necessarily the same commitments as those written down in a contract of employment. For example, the contract of employment will state the amount of pay an employee is to receive, but the psychological contract might include an expectation that the pay will be fair, or pay decisions will be reasonable. These ideas may change over time, and expectations may differ. The psychological contract is linked to employee engagement and levels of motivation. If an employee feels that their psychological contract has been breached, this may show up in that engagement or how they behave in the workplace every day.

ORGANIZATIONAL CULTURE

Organizational culture is another term used in HR and management that has a multitude of different definitions and perspectives. One of the most common ways to describe culture is 'how things are done around here'. It is generally considered to include how people behave at work, what it is like to work there, and beliefs and values. An organization that is considered a good place to work is sometimes described as having a good or positive culture. Culture is influenced by the work of HR and the day-to-day behaviours of people managers.

Employment law and employee relations

Employee relations and employment law are intertwined. Employment law governs much of the employment relationship, although these laws can look very different depending on the country and context. Typically, employment laws set minimum standards to which employers must adhere. These standards may relate to matters such as working hours, pay, holidays, breaks or workplace safety. They may also establish obligations upon the employer, such as to prevent discrimination or harassment. Laws often address both individual elements of the employment relationship, and the collective ones, with regulations about trade unions or collective action (discussed in Chapter 2). Some countries have very developed employment laws, whereas others take a much more minimalist approach, leaving more to the discretion of each employer.

HR professionals need to know the law and keep up to date with its development. Having a solid understanding of the employment law will allow you to provide quality advice and guidance, keep your organization compliant, reduce legal risk and ensure fair treatment for employees. As employment law is subject to change, especially when governments take different perspectives, staying informed is also crucial and should form part of the ongoing professional development of all HR professionals.

TIP

Identify ways that you can build your knowledge of employment law. Check out relevant, reputable websites or introductory books. Think about how you can keep this knowledge up to date – employment law changes regularly!

What is 'good' employee relations?

A positive employee relations climate is good for business. The UK Chartered Institute of Personnel and Development (CIPD) describe good employee relations as an organization that has high levels of employee involvement, commitment and engagement.[1] Through employee relations strategies (discussed in Chapter 8) organizations can build and maintain good working relationships with their people. In turn, this is good for the reputation of the organization and may contribute to attracting and retaining employees.

Good employee relations will also reduce the risk of conflict at work (the subject of Chapter 2) as well as the risk of legal claims against the organization.

Organizations define what 'good' employee relations looks like to them, depending on their goals, values, industry standards and workforce composition. This therefore varies from organization to organization. For some, it might be about reducing work-based conflict and legal risks. For others, it might align more closely to ideas about employee engagement and having a motivated, happy and satisfied workforce.

Employee relations is also aligned with ideas of 'good work', an idea of increasing interest to governments and campaigning organizations. The definition of good work usually includes strong employment protections, job security, fair wages and income security, good working conditions, inclusion and opportunity. Good work is believed to benefit employees and organizations, as well as society as a whole and the economy.

Good HR policies and practices can positively influence employee relations, especially through creating a strong employee experience. The UK CIPD suggests several ways to create positive employee relations, some of which we will explore as we go through this book. These include:

- Ensuring employees have ways to engage with employers, providing feedback either individually or through employee representatives.
- Having effective communication mechanisms to provide information to employees (voice).
- Providing training and guidance to people managers so that they can positively influence employee relations.
- Promoting a positive joint working culture, focusing on trust and building constructive relationships, especially with employee representatives.

STOP AND THINK

Consider your organization, even if you are not currently working in an HR role. Do you think there are good employee relations? What does this look like in your particular organizational context? How do you know employee relations are good – or bad?

The impact of 'bad' employee relations

Poor employee relations can lead to workplace conflict, a subject we will discuss in detail in Chapter 3. According to research by the CIPD employees who experience workplace conflict have lower levels of job satisfaction and are more likely to experience a negative impact on their mental or physical health.[2]

There is a significant financial cost too, when poor employee relations turns into conflict at work (see Chapter 2). According to research commissioned by Acas (the Advisory, Conciliation and Arbitration Service), the cost to employers of conflict in the workplace is £28.5 billion per annum.[3] The same research found that around 10 million people experienced conflict at work – this can result in a number of problems for businesses from stress to resignations and reduced productivity. Some forms of workplace conflict such as industrial action (explored in

Chapter 3) are especially problematic for organizations, resulting in potentially significant costs, lost productivity and impact on customers and service users.

Poor employee relations may also lead to grievances or complaints or even legal claims against an employer, either individual claims or collective ones. Legal claims are costly and time-consuming and may harm the organization's reputation if they become public knowledge.

Poor relations between employers and their employees may also result in reduced employee engagement and motivation. These are problematic outcomes for organizations, as employee engagement is associated with increased productivity, customer service and financial outcomes. Finally, bad employee relations might lead to employees leaving the organization or increased absenteeism.

There are therefore compelling reasons for organizations to foster good relations between them and the people that work for them.

The role of HR in employee relations

Some organizations may have specialists in employee relations, or even entire teams responsible for its scope. In other organizations, the typical work of employee relations, whether managing individual issues or the broader collective relationship, is within the remit of the HR generalist.

As an early career HR professional, you may find that you get involved in a range of different employee relations activities, some of which cross over with other typical HR work. When working with individual employees, this work might include the following:

- Advising on managing employee performance.
- Supporting managers with disciplinary matters.
- Hearing grievances (a form of dispute resolution)

- Absence management.
- Providing advice on policies and procedures.
- Helping to ensure compliance with employment laws.
- Managing employee relations (and legal) risks.

Depending on the organization, it might also include working with trade unions. We will now discuss some of these topics in more depth.

Policy formulation

Most organizations have policies or procedures that relate to how they employ people and address workplace issues. Examples include policies on attendance, conduct or behaviour – all of which we discuss in Chapters 4, 5 and 6. HR is often the owner of these policies, ensuring that they are legally compliant, support effective people management and help to create a positive employee experience.

Legal compliance

As we have already discussed, a great deal of the work of employee relations is governed by employment legislation. Employee relations includes ensuring that the organization and its managers are legally compliant in the way that employees are managed. HR professionals typically advise managers on the day-to-day application of employment law and are responsible for ensuring policies and processes are compliant.

Advice

Advice is central to the work of employee relations. This might involve providing employment law advice, as mentioned above. It may also include advising on employee relations good practice or the best way to handle a particular employee relations issue. Practically, it might mean explaining to a manager what they need to do or say when undertaking an absence meeting, hearing a grievance or conducting a disciplinary. Sometimes, this role also involves advising on people-related risks, such as the potential impact of new strategies, proposed change or decisions the organization is considering.

Dispute resolution

Also called conflict management, this refers to the process of resolving either individual complaints or collective issues that relate to a group of employees, up to formal industrial action. It is the subject of Chapter 3.

At a more senior level, employee relations might involve designing strategies to improve the relationship between employees and the organization. These often focus on the concepts we discussed earlier in this chapter, such as organizational culture, employee engagement, psychological contract and the employee experience. As well as employee relations specialist work, day-to-day HR practices influence wider employee relations as these practices contribute to a good employee experience.

The role of managers in employee relations

Just like the HR role, the role of managers in employee relations work varies. They may have a strategic role and make decisions about the organization that impact collective employee relations. They may also have an administrative, practical role, implementing policies and procedures in their everyday work. Most of the time, the employee's immediate manager is their most influential relationship in the workplace. The manager is essentially the 'face' of the organization to them.

Managers might do some of the following in employee relations work:

- Manage performance, including underperformance.
- Address issues relating to absence, conduct or behaviour.

- Administer, communicate and ensure compliance with people policies.
- Communication and engagement activity.
- Manage conflict in their team.

More senior leaders may also be involved in setting strategies that influence employee relations or take part in collective bargaining (discussed in Chapter 2). HR professionals often support managers through these different activities, providing advice and guidance. Managers will not necessarily have the capacity to keep up to date with good employment practices or changes in employment law and will often look to their HR partners to assist them with compliance.

Employee relations can be enhanced when HR professionals and people managers work together to improve communication, organizational culture and the overall employee experience.

Skills for employee relations

Employee relations, and indeed wider HR work, demands a broad range of skills. Some of these skills develop throughout a career, and not every early career HR professional will have all of them as they enter the profession.

In the Conclusion to this book, we plan how you can develop the skills you need to work in employee relations and some of these topics, such as conflict, are also explored in detail within this book. We begin our discussion by considering what skills are important, and how they are used in employee relations work.

Communication

It is common to have 'good communication skills' as a requirement for a job role, especially those within the field of HR. It is certainly a critical skill for those working in employee relations. Policies need to be well written so that they can be properly understood. Effective communication will support conflict management or dealing with sensitive situations. Clear communication is also important when delivering messages to employees and taking their feedback.

Emotional intelligence

Emotional intelligence is about how we recognize emotions in others and manage our own emotions. The nature of employee relations work makes emotional intelligence extremely important; people bring all sorts of complex emotions to work, especially when there is change, difficult issues or conflict at play. Employee relations work demands HR professionals to be excellent communicators, capable of using empathy while remaining calm under pressure. Being able to appreciate the feelings of others can help navigate the complexities of managing conflict.

Conflict management

Conflict, in some form or another, is almost inevitable in workplaces. People will not always get along or agree with one another, and they may disagree with the organization's actions. Managing conflict involves using a range of skills and techniques which we explore in depth in Chapter 3.

Resilience

Some elements of employee relations work are complex and challenging. From time to time, it can also be a high-pressure role, especially when dealing with difficult change or resolving disputes. Building resilience can help HR professionals, especially those early in their career, to handle these challenges effectively while staying well and avoiding stress.

Integrity

Arguably, integrity might be considered a quality or character trait rather than a skill, but as it can be developed and practised, and as it is important for employee relations work, we will consider it here. Integrity is concerned with acting ethically and having strong moral principles. It is also about being honest. Together, these form a strong basis for employee relations. While ideas about what constitutes good work and management might differ, HR professionals should be committed to ideas about fairness, equality and respect. The CIPD believes that HR professionals should be 'principle led' – going beyond what is legally required to do the right thing.[4]

Relationship management

Employee relations is, as the name suggests, all about relationships! There are relationships with employees, managers and leaders, and potentially trade unions or employee representatives. Relationship management skills will support some of the other skills discussed in this section – they will also help you to build trust and credibility with different stakeholders. Good relationships will help HR professionals get employee relations work done.

Coaching

Coaching is about helping people be resourceful and fulfil their potential. It usually involves encouraging people to reflect and come up with their own solutions to their challenges. While coaching is a formal qualification, having some basic coaching skills can help HR professionals to support managers develop all aspects of their people management skills.

Decision making

Sometimes in employee relations, there is not necessarily one 'right' answer. Decisions have to be balanced, taking into account costs, risks, legal requirements, employee engagement and experience and the needs of different stakeholders. While typically the final decision in an employee relations matter will rest with managers rather than HR, HR professionals may be called upon to give their opinion and advice. This may often involve setting out different available options, highlighting their pros and cons and making recommendations.

Risk management

Employee relations work often involves assessing and advising on risks. For example, legal risks associated with changes the organization wants to make or a risk that a particular decision will disengage or demotivate employees. Risks may then need to be minimized or mitigated.

EXERCISE

Undertake an initial review of your skills. Use the list of skills for employee relations in the previous section, reading more about them if you think this will aid your understanding. Use the following questions to help you reflect:

- Do you feel confident that any of the skills are a personal strength?

- Can you give examples of when you have demonstrated each of them?

- Can you recognize one skill that you need to develop? Identify an action that you can take to develop this skill.

Return to this skills list when you reach the Conclusion for more detailed reflection.

Common challenges in employee relations

In this section, we discuss some common challenges in employee relations, and how you can overcome these as an early career professional. We return to some of what we discuss here, such as managing employee complaints and working with trade unions, in more depth throughout this book.

Balancing different interests

A key challenge in all HR work is balancing the different needs and interests of key stakeholders. Some people see HR as a neutral 'middle ground' between management and employees, or even an employee support function. This is not usually the case. The organization employs HR professionals to support the achievement of its strategic goals through its people resources. Accordingly, HR should, generally, align its practices, programmes and initiatives to these goals. However, from time to time, what employees, managers or the broader organization want and need will come into conflict. For example, it might be good for employee relations to pay higher salaries to increase engagement, attraction and retention, but the organization may not be able to afford to do so. HR would then need to advise the business on risks and benefits; they may make recommendations, advise or even advocate for certain actions, but they are rarely the final decision maker.

Handling employee complaints

As we explore in Chapter 3, employees may raise concerns or complaints about matters relating to their work. These might be individual, relating only to them, or they might be collective, relating to a group of employees. Advising, managing and supporting managers with such complaints is part of the role of HR professionals. Sometimes employee complaints are relatively straightforward; they can also be complex, lengthy and involve sensitive, difficult issues. HR professionals need to know how to handle employee complaints fairly, following all relevant employment laws.

Understanding employment legislation

We've already discussed the critical need for HR and employee relations professionals to keep their legal knowledge up to date so that they can provide accurate advice to people managers. Employment legislation can be complex; it also changes and develops over time. When new laws are introduced, HR needs to first understand them and what they mean for their organization before potentially updating policies or processes, briefing people managers, and even changing ways of working if the legal changes are significant.

Managing difficult employee issues

We explore this subject in depth in later chapters, particularly Chapter 7. HR professionals often deal with every single aspect of employing people in practice. Employees can get ill or bereaved, have personal problems, underperform, behave poorly or become involved in conflict. HR professionals need to understand how to manage these complex situations, in line with legislation and good practice, advising and coaching people managers to do the same.

Working with trade unions

Working with trade unions is a key part of employee relations. As we explore in Chapter 2, not every organization formally recognizes trade unions, but even if they do not, employees may themselves choose to be members. Working collaboratively with trade unions is an important skill for HR professionals and employee relations specialists.

Dealing with 'difficult' employees

The term 'difficult employee' is a loaded one. Some people might consider a person 'difficult' when they are raising legitimate concerns or problems. Employees labelled as 'difficult' might be advocating for change or improvements, perhaps to those who are resistant to change. However, some people can, regardless of the reason, be quite challenging to work with. Effective employee relations work requires the ability to collaborate and communicate with all sorts of people who have unique complexities, emotions and perspectives. HR professionals may sometimes need to suspend judgement or put aside personal feelings – or frustrations!

Ensuring consistency

Consistency is another balancing act for HR. To ensure fairness, it is often appropriate to treat similar issues that arise at work in the same way. For example, if two employees demonstrate the same sort of poor behaviour in the workplace, it would often be fair and reasonable to treat them similarly. However, there might well be circumstances where it *is* appropriate to take different action, perhaps because there are mitigating circumstances. This is often a judgement call and will require HR professionals to consider the different options carefully and assess risks before offering advice.

Keeping pace with the changing nature of work

The world of work is always changing. Since the Covid-19 pandemic, there has been a global rise in remote and hybrid work, as well as an increased interest in other forms of flexible working, such as the four-day week. Remote work allows employers to hire workers all over the world, not just those in their localities.

'Gig' working and self-employment are also rising, where workers engage with employers on a much more flexible and often short-term basis. At the same time, technological change is advancing rapidly with digitalization and artificial intelligence (AI) reshaping how organizations work. These new technologies will fundamentally change jobs; some jobs may disappear, while others will be created. To work with these changing technologies, employees need to develop a range of new skills. Employment laws will also continue to change and develop, influenced by some of the trends discussed here as well as new research and ideas and the political positions of governments.

These trends, combined with the other external influences that always affect organizations, mean that the relationship between employers and employees will continue to evolve and reshape. They might even create new grounds for workplace conflict. On a practical level, the changing face of work might mean new everyday ways of working. More broadly, it will include how organizations employ workers and how they communicate with, develop, involve and manage them.

As an early-career HR professional, you need to keep up to date, keep learning new skills, look to the external environment and translate these trends for leaders in your organizations.

STOP AND THINK

Reflect on your organization, whether you are currently in an HR role or not. Can you identify any trends or changes specific to your industry or the roles that people undertake, that might influence employee relations now or in the future?

CHAPTER SUMMARY

- Employee relations is a broad term that describes the relationship between organizations and their employees. It includes the individual relationship between an employee and the organization and the collective relationship – the organization and employees as a whole.

- Employee relations and employment law are intertwined, and legislation governs many aspects of employee relations in practice. Early career HR professionals should build a working knowledge of up-to-date local legislation to be effective in their roles.

- Good employee relations is important for an organization's reputation, to attract and retain employees and reduce the chance of workplace conflict.

- The HR role within employee relations is a broad one; HR professionals may advise and support on practical matters such as handling grievances or legal compliance, work with trade unions, or lead employee relations strategies.

- To be effective in the field of employee relations, early career HR professionals need to build skills in conflict management, communication and collaboration, emotional intelligence and relationship management. They will also benefit from a working knowledge of relevant academic theories.

- There are several challenges you might encounter in employee relations, such as balancing the interests of employees, managers and the organization, handling complaints, dealing with trade unions and 'difficult' people. You will also need to keep pace with the changing nature of work and what that means for your employee relations work.

REVIEW QUESTIONS

1 Explain why it is important for HR professionals to understand employment legislation.

2 Name three benefits of positive employee relations.

3 Define what is meant by 'collective employee relations'.

4 List five skills that you will need to be effective in employee relations work.

- Name three common challenges of employee relations work and identify one way that each of these can be overcome.

Further reading

Aylott, E (2022) *Employee Relations: A practical introduction*, Kogan Page

CIPD, The profession map, https://www.cipd.org/globalassets/media/comms/the-people-profession/profession-map-pdfs/full-standards-download-a4-2024/ (archived at https://perma.cc/F22S-PE7A)

Endnotes

1 CIPD (2024) Employee relations: An introduction, https://www.cipd.org/uk/knowledge/factsheets/relations-employees-factsheet/ (archived at https://perma.cc/NM2A-GT8E)

2 CIPD (2024) CIPD Good Work Index, https://www.cipd.org/uk/knowledge/reports/goodwork/ (archived at https://perma.cc/HY3L-M9H5)

3 Acas (2021) Independent research: Estimating the costs of workplace conflict, https://www.acas.org.uk/research-and-commentary/estimating-the-costs-of-workplace-conflict/report (archived at https://perma.cc/T632-7H2C)

4 CIPD, The Profession Map, https://www.cipd.org/uk/the-people-profession/the-profession-map/explore-the-profession-map/ (archived at https://perma.cc/755Z-Q97J)

CHAPTER TWO

Collective employee relations

Introduction

This chapter focuses on the collective dimension of employee relations, discussing the relationship between the organization and their employees as a group. As collective employee relations are often conducted through employee representatives or formal structures such as trade unions and collective bargaining, we explore these connected elements, including practical guidance on how HR professionals can work effectively with trade union representatives. We also consider different forms of employee involvement and participation, discussing the importance of engaging with employees on matters that affect them at work.

Some of the areas discussed in this chapter are typically covered by employment legislation, which varies from country to country. This chapter does not seek to summarize the law; HR professionals should always check the requirements that apply to them wherever they work, especially before proceeding with formal consultation.

LEARNING OBJECTIVES

By the end of this chapter, you will be able to:

- Explain what is meant by collective employment relations.
- Describe what employee involvement and participation are, and list ways they can be done.
- Define the role of trade unions in collective employment relations and collective bargaining, and identify relevant skills needed by HR professionals when working with trade unions.
- Understand the benefits and drawbacks of collective bargaining.

Introducing collective employee relations

Collective employee relations refers to the relationship between the organization and groups of its employees. A group can be defined either as one whole cohort or as smaller specific groups. This contrasts with the relationship between the organization and individual employees, regarding their performance, behaviour, conduct and attendance. There is sometimes a tension between the individual relationship and the collective one.

A range of factors influences what collective employee relations 'looks like' in any particular context, including the organization's size, overall culture, history and the type of work that people do. Collective aspects of the employment relationship, which vary from organization to organization, include discussing or negotiating on terms and conditions of employment, as well as engaging with employees about those things that affect them in the workplace.

The collective relationship is often managed through engaging with employee representatives or groups, including trade unions. There might be statutory (legally required) elements to collective employee relations or voluntary ones, where organizations have entered into agreements with trade unions or worker organizations. Legal frameworks may accompany some of the activities associated with collective employee relations; some countries have employment laws around trade union recognition, industrial action and consultation and negotiation.

TIP

Undertake some research to ensure you are familiar with relevant legal frameworks and regulations surrounding collective employee relations in your region. If you work for a global organization, this may mean navigating different requirements in different countries.

Collective employee relations plays a crucial role in shaping workplace culture and influencing employee engagement. The way organizations interact with trade unions, employee representatives, and workers as a collective group can have significant implications for employee trust, motivation and the psychological contract. An organization's competitive advantage may lie with its people, and their skills, knowledge and experience. A well-managed collective employee relations approach fosters mutual trust between employees and employers, making it vitally important to leaders and HR professionals alike.

Employee involvement and participation

The term 'employee involvement and participation' describes methods for including employees in decisions that affect their work or the organization they work for. The term includes formal consultation or negotiation with employee representatives when this is provided through legal processes or collective agreements, but it also includes all sorts of other methods. There is a crossover between involvement and participation and employee voice (defined in Chapter 1), although voice is often more about listening to employees' thoughts and opinions rather than their active involvement or influence over decision making.

Involvement and participation can take place directly with employees or through collective representatives. In practice, many organizations do elements of both. In the past, and as we shall see in the discussion on trade unions later in this chapter, a great deal of activity that relates to involvement and participation was undertaken through trade unions. This is no longer necessarily the case.

Examples of employee involvement and participation could include:

- Employee surveys focused either on the organization as a whole or on specific issues.
- Committees with employee representation, such as a safety or wellbeing committee.
- Quality circles, where small groups of employees meet regularly to discuss and solve work-related issues and challenges.
- Employees as board representatives, taking part in issues like corporate governance.
- Focus groups, exploring specific issues from the employee perspective.
- Suggestion schemes or platforms that allow employees to make proposals for improvement directly to the organization and its managers.

TIP

In the UK, organizations are sometimes legally required to consult with employees, for example, when there are proposals for redundancy or when transferring employees to another employer. This usually involves providing information on proposals before seeking formal input from employees. There are specific rules around how this form of involvement and participation should be conducted; always familiarize yourself with these if you are advising on these activities.

Many benefits can be gained from employee involvement and participation. Actively engaging employees in decision-making or workplace improvements can help them feel valued, thereby increasing motivation and job satisfaction. Involvement can also help to foster a sense of ownership and accountability on the part of employees. On a practical level, organizations can benefit from diverse perspectives and firsthand knowledge of workplace issues, which may lead to new ideas. Effective methods for employee voice, involvement and participation can also reduce workplace conflict. Research has found benefits of involvement and participation also include:

- improved organizational performance
- increased employee commitment
- employee motivation and positive organizational culture[1]

Before employees can be properly involved, they first need to be informed. This means that the organization needs to provide sufficient information about what is going on in the business, how it is performing against objectives or targets and any potential future changes. Exactly what and how much information is provided varies from organization to organization, as will the methods for sharing it. As we shall see in Chapter 8, some organizations have internal teams responsible for communicating directly to employees. Examples of employee information might include:

- newsletters, email roundups or magazines
- leader communications such as blogs, emails or videos
- intranets, online hubs or internal social media platforms
- business or strategy updates

- events, such as meetings or forums
- social media platforms

STOP AND THINK

Reflect on your organization, whether you are currently in an HR role or not.

- Which different methods for employee involvement and participation can you identify?

- How effective do you think the current employee involvement and participation methods are, and what impact do you think they have on your collective employee relations?

Where organizations work with trade unions and their representatives, there is likely to be a degree of formal structure around involvement and participation approaches. This might include regular meetings, agreements to share information such as those that will facilitate collective bargaining (discussed in the next section) and facilities for representatives.

Trade Unions

Trade Union: A formal organization that works on behalf of its members to improve terms and conditions in the workplace.

A BRIEF HISTORY OF TRADE UNIONS

The origins of trade unions can be traced back to early craft guilds that sought to protect the interests of skilled workers. However, trade unions as we know them today largely emerged during the Industrial Revolution and the introduction of the factory system. Harsh conditions and low wages in these workplaces created the conditions for trade unionism to flourish. There were few of the workplace protections that we are familiar with today available for workers.

Many employers were opposed to trade unions and various attempts, including legislation, were made to prevent employees from organizing. Employers did not wish to have restrictions placed upon their ability to do as they pleased in relation to the people that worked for them. Eventually, sometimes after long campaigns, many industrialized countries permitted trade unions to exist with the introduction of various forms of legislation.

Trade union membership grew from the early 1900s. In the UK, membership peaked in the late 1970s with over 13 million trade union members across all industries. During this time, industrial action in the form of strikes was a common occurrence, which caused political concerns. Shortly after this period, new laws were introduced to curb trade union power, which some people felt had become too great. Many of these laws remain in place today.

Over the last few decades, trade union membership has declined significantly, partly because some of the industries in which it was highly embedded, such as coal mining and manufacturing, have also declined. Today, union membership and recognition are often concentrated in certain industries and job types, but nonetheless trade unions remain an important part of employee relations in many countries.

In many parts of the world, employees have a legal right to join a trade union. They normally pay a monthly fee to be a member, which entitles them to a range of benefits, including representation for any workplace issues they might experience. Employees can also choose not to join a trade union. Generally, employees cannot be penalized for their decision either way. One of the principal activities of trade unions is collective bargaining.

Collective bargaining: Where a trade union or employee organization negotiates with employers on behalf of their members, often on matters of pay and benefits.

The focus of collective bargaining is often terms and conditions of employment, especially pay, but it often extends further than that too. Like many of the subjects in this book, collective bargaining (and indeed trade union representation) is governed by relevant employment legislation. Alongside the decline in trade union membership, there has been a similar decline in the number of employees whose terms and conditions of employment are covered by collective bargaining. As the name suggests, collective bargaining is based on the collective – it assumes that employees coming together to seek improvement in their work or conditions have greater power and influence than a single employee acting individually. We will discuss collective bargaining further later in this chapter.

Employers can choose whether or not to 'recognize' a trade union; this refers to entering into a formal written agreement with the union for representation which sets out the scope of the recognition. When they do so, essentially, the trade union influences the relationship between the employee and the employer. Often, a written agreement (sometimes called a recognition agreement) will set out the scope of the recognition and any important principles about how the trade union and organization will work together and what topics will be the subject of consultation or negotiation.

When a trade union is recognized, they gain a range of rights to act on behalf of their members. These rights include:

- a right to accompany employees to meetings, such as grievance or disciplinary hearings
- paid time off to do their work as a representative and attend training related to their role
- to be provided with information about the organization that will help them to consult and negotiate
- protection from experiencing any detriment at work relating to their role as an employee representative

- access to facilities that help them to undertake their role as a representative, such as meeting rooms or communication technologies

In the UK, most trade union recognition and collective bargaining are voluntary, although there are circumstances in which employers can be required to recognize a trade union if enough employees wish them to do so. This can involve a complex process that includes a ballot of employees.

STOP AND THINK

Reflect on your organization. Does it recognize a trade union, or have any formal processes for consulting with employee representatives? If yes, do you know what those agreements include? If possible, review a copy of the agreement.

Trade unions usually have specific legal protections, as do their representatives. The term 'trade union representative' includes full-time employees of the union itself, or your own employees who have been through a formal process to become a representative. They will do their representative work alongside their normal job for you.

The relationships between trade unions and the organizations that recognize them vary considerably, and might exist on a spectrum from very co-operative to adversarial. This may vary over time depending on the people involved, or what is happening within the organization that affects the members of trade unions. Ideally, the aim is for co-operative, mutually beneficial relationships with recognized trade unions, but this is not always possible as situations will arise where the interests of the organization and employees are opposed. We will discuss some of these more complex situations in our chapters on conflict at work and managing difficult issues.

> **TIP**
>
> Acas has a series of guides that provide information on working with trade unions. Search for these guides and review them to improve your knowledge of good practice in this area.

Working with trade unions

As we discussed in the previous chapter, the role of the HR professional within employee relations is a broad one which varies from organization to organization. HR professionals and managers need to have the skills to work with trade union representatives when an organization formally recognizes them – and sometimes even if they do not. Important skills for working effectively with trade unions include communication, relationship building, conflict resolution and problem-solving.

Depending on the organization and the form of recognition that has been agreed, HR professionals may find themselves working with trade union representatives in a variety of ways:

- Attending meetings with individual employees, such as discipline or grievance hearings, where the employee is represented by a trade union official.
- Consulting with employee representatives on changes or projects that affect employees in the workplace (such as some of those discussed in Chapter 7).
- Developing people policies that will be consulted upon with trade unions.
- Taking part in collective bargaining discussions, or formal consultation required by law, such as when redundancies or transfers are proposed.
- Managing collective disputes such as industrial action (discussed in Chapter 3).

It is not only HR professionals who need to have good relationships with trade unions – managers at all levels of the organization do too. Managers and leaders may also be involved in many of the aspects of employee relations discussed here, such as attending meetings, engaging in collective bargaining discussions or negotiation and consultation. Where organizations formally recognize unions or where they are very involved in organizational life, it may be important to include relevant skills in management development programmes.

As explained in the box about the history of trade unions, membership and recognition in the UK has declined in recent years. This means that not all managers (especially those from non-union backgrounds) will have experience in how to manage these crucial relationships and may look to HR for guidance and advice. You may find it helpful to ensure managers are aware of the rights and responsibilities of trade union representatives, especially if they are going to be involved in meetings where they will be present. Where unions are formally recognized, managers will benefit from building strong working relationships with representatives.

If you need to consult or negotiate with a trade union (or provide advice or guidance to managers who do), you might find some of these tips from the CIPD helpful:

- Be flexible and look for areas of common interest. Aim for a 'win-win' scenario where both parties can see some successes.
- Before entering into any consultation or negotiation, be clear about what you would like to achieve from it – what does success look like?
- You might not always be able to gain everything you want in a negotiation. Have an idea about where you can compromise.
- Listen carefully and remember that whatever the issue under discussion, you need to maintain a constructive long-term relationship with your trade union.[2]

> **TIP**
>
> As not all organizations formally recognize trade unions, it can be difficult for early career HR professionals to gain experience in this important area of employee relations. See if you can identify any opportunities to gain experience in working with trade unions – even if you do not formally recognize a trade union, their representatives may still accompany employees to disciplinary or grievance meetings.
>
> • Ask if you can attend any collective bargaining or consultation meetings if you have them.
> • Volunteer to support managers in meetings where trade union representatives are present, even if it is just as a note-taker.
> • Talk to more experienced colleagues about their experiences of working with trade unions and their representatives.

If you do have to work with trade union representatives, some of the following practical tips might help you to ensure success:

• Understand the legal framework that relates to any of your discussions. Make sure you understand any relevant legislation or codes of practice.
• Know your collective agreement, if you have one. Make sure you are clear on its scope and provisions and the rights that it affords employee representatives.
• Build positive relationships with trade union representatives. This will help to ensure long-term success and give you a platform for effective dialogue.
• Act with integrity. Your personal behaviours will support effective relationships. Even when you do not agree, having a reputation for personal integrity will serve you well as an HR professional.

- Engage in active listening – seek to understand the views and interests of representatives and their members.
- Prepare for meetings, especially where you need to consult or negotiate. Think about what the trade union might be seeking and do your research on the topic. Consider what position they may take and how you will respond.

The importance of good relations with a trade union cannot be underestimated. It helps change to run smoothly, reduces the risk of conflict or disputes, and increases the likelihood of you working together for the mutual benefit of the organization and its employees.

European Works Councils (EWC)

Trade unions are not the only form of representation in the workplace. European Works Councils are bodies representing the European employees of a company. Where an organization has more than 1000 employees in European Economic Areas (EEA), employees may request that a European Works Council is established (since Brexit, this doesn't include UK employees, although any agreements put in place before Brexit may continue).

The purpose of a European Works Council is to inform and consult employees about their employment or working conditions. It's very similar to the purpose of a trade union. Just like trade unions, representatives and members of European Works Councils have certain rights and responsibilities.

TIP

The rules around creating European Works Councils can be quite complicated – always check the rules that apply in the country where you work.

Non-union representation

Sometimes, an organization may want to support employee involvement and participation, but not want to formally recognize a trade union or set up (if eligible) a European Works Council. It may prefer something less formal or not wish to have representatives with as many legal rights and responsibilities. An alternative is for organizations to set up their own employee forums or committees, which may be general committees or have a specific remit. Such employee forums might operate on an ongoing basis or could be established for a time-limited purpose, such as to discuss a particular project or initiative.

In those cases where organizations are required by law to consult with employees and where a trade union is not already recognized, they may need to set up a representative group just for this purpose. These representatives will also have rights and responsibilities, even though they are not formally recognized in the same way as a trade union.

Collective bargaining

As we have already seen, one of the main functions of trade unions is collective bargaining. Usually, an organization has a written agreement with their trade union setting out how any negotiations between the organization and the union will be conducted. These agreements might detail what sort of things representatives will be consulted upon, such as pay, how often meetings will take place, and what will happen if the two parties cannot reach any agreement during negotiations. They might also detail mechanisms for resolving workplace disputes.

Through collective bargaining, collective agreements can be made. Usually, when an agreement has been made through collective bargaining, such as the size of an annual pay rise, this applies to all employees who work for the organization, not just the members of the trade union with whom it has been agreed.

Some collective bargaining takes place at a national level. For example, some sectors such as Higher Education, negotiate collectively with the trade union to secure collective bargaining rights for all employees. This is sometimes known as centralized bargaining (as opposed to decentralized bargaining, which refers to discussions that take place at a local level).

There are potential benefits and drawbacks to undertaking collective bargaining, especially to determine terms and conditions of employment. It can provide a structured framework for negotiating terms, and employees feel that they have a voice in the process. Employment terms are standardized, and pay disparities are reduced. However, pay negotiations can sometimes be complex and lengthy. Employment terms, especially pay, can become quite rigid, potentially making it more difficult for employers to adapt quickly to economic fluctuations or industry changes. It may also mean that employees cannot be rewarded for their personal contribution or performance, if pay is set the same for everyone. For some employees, this might be demotivating, or it might not allow organizations to attract the best talent. If agreements cannot be reached with unions through collective bargaining, conflict may result, as we shall see in Chapter 3.

Accordingly, whether collective bargaining is the 'right' strategy for any organization will depend on a variety of factors, including its industry, workforce composition, business objectives and existing employee relations climate.

TIP

If you undertake collective bargaining with a trade union, and this is responsible for setting employee terms and conditions of employment, this should be stated in the employee's contract of employment. Check what your contracts say about collective bargaining, if anything.

EXERCISE

Review employment legislation wherever you are based. Research when organizations are required by employment legislation to consult or negotiate collectively with trade unions or employee groups. Make a list.

CHAPTER SUMMARY

- Collective employee relations, especially consultation with employees, is often governed by legislation. HR professionals should therefore ensure that they have an overview of relevant legal requirements in their own countries.

- Employee participation and involvement is a term that refers to the different ways that organizations include employees in decisions that affect their work or the organization they work for. It includes collective bargaining, informing employees about the organization and employee voice activities.

- Trade unions are organizations that work on behalf of their members to improve terms and conditions at work – this often takes place through collective bargaining on terms and conditions of employment.

- HR professionals need a range of skills to work effectively with trade unions, including communication, relationship building, conflict resolution and problem-solving. Early career HR professionals should look for opportunities to work with trade unions to build their experience.

REVIEW QUESTIONS

1 What is a trade union? Write a definition that summarizes your understanding of the purpose of a trade union and what they do in practice.

2 Summarize your understanding of collective bargaining. What would a collective bargaining agreement typically contain?

3 Name three different ways that an organization can ensure employee involvement and participation.

4 Make a list of activities that early career HR professionals might undertake when working with trade unions.

Further reading

Acas, Trade union representation in the workplace, https://www.acas.org.uk/sites/default/files/2021-03/trade-union-representation-in-the-workplace.pdf (archived at https://perma.cc/XDQ2-VU4W)

Aylott, E (2022) *Employment Law: A practical introduction*, Kogan Page

Endnotes

1 Gifford, J, Neathey, F and Loukas, G (2005) Employee involvement: Information, consultation and discretion, Institue for Employment Studies, https://www.employment-studies.co.uk/system/files/resources/files/427.pdf (archived at https://perma.cc/2NBD-YB3U)

2 CIPD (2025) Collective bargaining and negotiating with trade unions, https://www.cipd.org/uk/knowledge/guides/working-trade-unions/#collective-bargaining (archived at https://perma.cc/W9G2-YKD7)

CHAPTER THREE

Conflict at work

Introduction

This chapter considers different perspectives on workplace conflict and explores how it is managed at both an individual and collective level. In practice, an early career professional is likely to focus on supporting people managers with individual conflict, such as grievances or complaints. We therefore consider this area in detail, including practical tips and common challenges. We also discuss the impact of conflict on the workplace and its potential outcomes, as well as forms of collective conflict such as industrial action.

LEARNING OBJECTIVES

By the end of this chapter, you will be able to:

- Explain the difference between the pluralist and unitarist perspectives of conflict at work.
- Describe the different forms that conflict at work can take.
- Explain different ways that conflict can be managed.
- Describe what is meant by an employee grievance, and explain how an organization should address one.
- Give examples of collective conflict and identify methods to resolve and prevent it.

Perspectives on conflict at work

Conflict at work can arise for all sorts of reasons and present itself in many different ways. Some people believe that conflict in the employee relationship is inevitable because the relationship is inherently unbalanced, and employees and managers have different interests and goals. This is known as a 'pluralist' perspective, which assumes that conflict will always exist, and the role of employee relations is to manage and minimize that conflict. Conflict is not necessarily seen as a problem within the pluralist perspective, as it can help to bring about change.

The contrary perspective is known as the 'unitarist' viewpoint. Instead of focusing on the differences between employees and employers, this perspective focuses on what they have in common. For example, both employees and employers benefit from the success of the overall organization. Those who believe in the unitarist perspective reject the idea that there has to be conflict within the employment relationship – in fact, conflict is seen as disruptive and something to be avoided. This point of view is much closer to contemporary ideas about human resource management, especially employee engagement. Within this perspective, trade unions are seen as unnecessary or even disruptive.

Both perspectives are evident in human resource management and the work of HR professionals. When conflict does exist, whether individual or collective, processes to address this conflict are necessary. Often, these are prescribed by employment law or formal guidance. Similarly, human resource management also seeks to improve the employment experience through improving work and workplaces, and activities incorporating employee engagement, employee experience and through the employment lifecycle.

STOP AND THINK

Which of these perspectives do you think is true of the workplace? Why do you think this? Explain your position and rationale.

Forms of conflict

The term 'conflict' suggests arguments, disagreements or clashes. This can be true, but in practice in the workplace, it can encompass a range of activities, emotions and manifestations. Conflict can occur between the organization and its employees, between different teams or groups, or between employees themselves. Conflict can be formal (organized) or informal (unorganized). We've already discussed some forms of formal conflict, such as industrial action, in Chapter 2. Conflict at work can include:

- formal industrial action, such as strikes or stoppages of work
- employee absence or turnover
- grievances or complaints
- personality clashes
- sabotage, disobedience or workplace deviance
- withdrawal of co-operation or effort

STOP AND THINK

Reflect on your own experiences. Have you ever witnessed any conflict at work? If so, what form did it take, and how did the organization respond?

Managing Conflict

Just as there is formal and informal conflict, conflict may be managed formally or informally. The process of managing conflict is sometimes known as 'dispute resolution'. The approach needed to address any particular conflict will depend on the issue, whether it is collective or individual, any relevant employment laws and the goals of the organization. There is often no 'right or wrong' way to manage conflict at work, only the most appropriate one for the circumstances. Some forms of conflict, such as individual complaints, may need to be addressed through internal processes or policies.

In this chapter, we will discuss both individual and collective conflict. Both of these have several factors in common:

- Early intervention is key to preventing issues from escalating or becoming entrenched.
- HR professionals are typically involved at most stages in managing conflict, so it's an important area of skill to develop.
- Conflict needs to be managed following relevant local employment legislation.
- The manager's role in managing conflict is key.

Not all managers, however, find this an easy task. Some may lack confidence due to inexperience in managing conflict. Research has also found that managers are concerned about the workload of conflict management (especially when procedures might be time-consuming), the impact of conflict on employee wellbeing, and the risk of employment litigation.[1]

Managers should be trained to manage conflict effectively. Training should include legal aspects of conflict management, options for dispute resolution and how to navigate tricky issues. HR professionals can act as guides, coaches and sources of specialist advice.

In practice, early career HR professionals are most likely to be involved with managing individual conflict, so we begin by looking at different forms of individual conflict and how they can be addressed.

Individual conflict – employee grievances

Employee complaints and concerns are often referred to as grievances. An employee can raise a grievance about any aspect of their employment, from their working conditions to matters relating to pay or benefits.

> **Grievance procedure/policy:** A formal process used by an organization to address and resolve employee complaints or concerns.

It is important to take all grievances seriously. Most organizations have some form of process or procedure for dealing with individual grievances, although these often differ from the processes used to address collective conflict. Internal policies and relevant employment legislation should always be followed when hearing individual grievances.

It is common for grievance processes or procedures to have both informal and formal elements. Most organizations encourage people to resolve differences informally if they can, rather than resort to formal processes, which can be time-consuming and stressful.

Informal resolution

Informal resolution often begins with an employee having a conversation with their immediate manager to see if a problem can be resolved. Sometimes this is possible, but depending on the nature of the complaint, the issue might be outside the manager's control or influence.

When issues can be addressed locally and informally, this is usually quicker and stops an issue from becoming protracted. If a grievance cannot be resolved informally, it can be raised formally.

> TIP
>
> Sometimes employees feel that they can't raise an issue informally, or it would not be appropriate to do so. For example, if they feel that they are being bullied or harassed, it might be more appropriate for a grievance to be managed (and also recorded)

through the formal grievance procedure. Employees should not
be required to go through the informal process if they do not
wish to.

Mediation

Mediation: A voluntary process through which a trained and
neutral third party (the mediator) works with employees to
resolve disputes or conflicts in the workplace.

Mediation is another form of informal dispute resolution that is
often used when there is conflict between two or more individuals. Although it isn't formal, it is structured. The process typically
includes an initial meeting with each party to understand their
perspectives, followed by a joint session where they discuss the
issues and explore possible solutions. Whereas a grievance
procedure usually involves some sort of investigation into what
has happened and a judgement about whether someone or
something is right or wrong, mediation focuses on collaboration
and mutual problem-solving. The aim is to work through issues
and agree ways to work in the future.

TIP

Mediation is voluntary and confidential. No one should be
required or pressured to engage in mediation if they are not fully
committed to the idea. This would undermine the purpose of
mediation, and any agreements made are unlikely to last.

There are many benefits of mediation. It can be less stressful and
less time-consuming than a formal grievance procedure. If used
at an early stage, it can prevent conflicts from escalating. While
mediation agreements might involve some compromise, it can

help preserve the personal relationships between the parties and it is less likely that someone will have to feel like they 'lost'.

Despite the benefits, mediation is not suitable for all situations. It is important to consider power dynamics; mediation might not be suitable between a senior manager and a much more junior employee, as the employee might not feel that they can speak openly and honestly, or might be concerned about the impact on their career. It might also not be appropriate if the complaint is about harassment, bullying or discrimination. These might be better addressed through the proper procedures – if harassment or bullying is occurring, disciplinary procedures may be necessary.

WHAT WOULD YOU DO?
Number 1

Review the following scenario. Would you recommend mediation for this situation? Explain the reasons for your answer.

An employee and a manager both talk to you separately about an issue they are experiencing with each other. The manager feels that the employee is unnecessarily difficult and argumentative, and provides examples of them pushing back when they ask them to complete work or chase them for late work. The employee tells you that their manager is micro-managing them, singling them out for criticism, and constantly chasing them for work before the deadline. The employee clearly states that they feel they are being bullied.

The HR role in addressing grievances

HR professionals may undertake a range of roles in relation to the grievance process. First, they need to ensure that any grievances are considered properly, in line with process and treated with confidentiality where appropriate. They might also provide advice on options for addressing grievances, such as the suitability of different solutions or forms of dispute resolution.

HR professionals often attend grievance hearings to support managers and advise on how complaints should be investigated, if this is required.

In contrast, the role of the manager is to meet with the employee to understand their concern, undertake any necessary investigation into the issue raised, and ultimately to decide on whether or not the complaint is valid.

TIP

Grievances can be a source of insight into employee relations in your organization. If you have a lot of grievances, or several grievances about the same issues, this might suggest underlying problems that need the attention of management or HR. Check whether your organization records and analyses grievances from employees, and if there are any trends in those complaints.

Handling grievances

If a concern cannot be resolved informally, the next step is to initiate a formal process. Always address any grievances received promptly. Begin by acknowledging that the grievance has been received, and then put together a plan for how the complaint will be considered. The person who 'receives' the grievance may or may not be the right person to 'hear' or review it, especially if they are in some way involved or need to provide input into any investigation.

STOP AND THINK

Consider your organization and its culture. Do you think it would be easy for an employee to speak up about workplace concerns? Do you feel that your employees believe their concerns would be listened to and acted upon?

Grievance meetings, often also called hearings, are usually held in response to a received complaint. The purpose of a grievance meeting is usually to hear what the employee has to say so that the complaint can be properly considered or investigated further. The initial meeting is not usually to provide a response or decision.

Grievances will usually need to be investigated to see if they have merit. This needs to be done thoroughly and fairly. An appointed manager usually hears the grievance. The grievance hearing manager should be independent – it may or may not be appropriate for it to be the manager of the employee who has raised the grievance, depending on this issue.

Exactly what needs to be included in an investigation will depend on the issue, but could include some of the following:

- Interviewing any witnesses.
- Interviewing the employee's manager.
- Reviewing internal policies, records or documents.

TIP

Once the investigation is finalized, it is a good idea for the investigating manager to write a summary report of what they have found and the decision that has been made. This ensures a full record that could be important for the future, especially if the employee is not satisfied with the outcome and wishes to take the matter further. The employee who raised the grievance should be provided with a copy of the report.

Outcomes from grievances

We usually talk about a grievance being 'upheld' or not upheld. If a grievance is upheld, this means that the complaint is agreed upon. The employee's concerns are found to be valid, and usually an attempt will be made to address them or put things right. If a grievance is upheld, a resolution should be put in place to address the concern – this will depend on the nature of the grievance. It is typical during earlier meetings to ask an employee what resolution they seek.

Sometimes, the outcome of a grievance might be that another formal process has to begin. For example, if an employee raises a grievance that says they have been harassed by a colleague and this is found to be true, it may be necessary to begin disciplinary proceedings against that individual. We look at how you would do this in Chapter 5.

Employees usually have the right to appeal the outcomes of a grievance hearing. They might raise an appeal that relates to the process or the decision. Appeals should be heard by an independent manager who has not previously been involved with the issue.

TIP

Remember, raising a grievance can be a difficult and stressful experience. Sometimes, an issue will have been a problem for a long time before an employee feels that they need to raise it formally. It can also be a difficult experience for other employees who may be required to input into the grievance investigation, perhaps as witnesses. Make sure you build wellbeing support into your approach for handling grievances.

Grievance procedures are important; they can help people find resolutions to their issues at work. They are a form of employee voice, and can act as a way to bring serious problems to light. However, having or undertaking a process does not necessarily mean that issues are resolved, as we will explore later in this chapter when we look at common challenges in managing grievances.

Grievance procedures in themselves do not necessarily ensure good relationships between employees; after a process has been concluded, whatever the outcome, the people involved often have to continue working together. Grievance procedures can also make positions more entrenched. Employees become emotionally invested in their stated positions and may be unwilling to let them go or compromise. It may be necessary after a grievance procedure to help people re-establish effective working relationships. Mediation is sometimes used for this purpose, too.

WHAT WOULD YOU DO?
Number 2

An employee has formally raised a grievance to a senior manager regarding what they feel is unfair treatment by their immediate manager. The employee claims that they've been subjected to constant criticism about their work, exclusion from meetings and a lack of support. They think that the manager wants them to leave, and they have provided a diary detailing the incidents of unfair treatment.

- What would you recommend to the senior manager? How should this matter be handled?
- What evidence would need to be gathered to consider this grievance fully?
- What action would you take if the grievance were found to be true?

Dos and don'ts for HR in grievance meetings

DO

- Remain impartial. Even if you have a view on the grievance based on your perspectives or beliefs, during the process it is important to be open-minded and neutral when considering the grievance.
- Take detailed notes of the discussion and make sure that everyone is provided with a copy after the meeting.

- Explain the purpose of the meeting and the process that will be followed at the beginning.
- Give the employee time to fully explain their concern or state their case.
- Investigate the grievance. After hearing the employee's concerns, it will usually be necessary to take time to review what has been said and possibly conduct an investigation into any points made.
- Ask the employee what resolution they are seeking to resolve their grievance. Discussing this does not mean that you are compelled to agree, but it is important to understand what they are hoping to achieve.

DON'T

- Allow emotions to impact the meeting. If anyone gets upset or emotional, it may be appropriate to take a short break – as the HR representative, it is fine for you to call for an adjournment.
- Make an immediate decision. Even if the issue is a straightforward one and you feel you can answer it quickly, take time to reflect and check whether any additional investigation is needed before making a final call.
- Be drawn into a debate or discussion on the issue or giving your opinion. The purpose of a grievance meeting is to understand the employee's concern or complaint.
- Neglect to follow up and support employees after the grievance is concluded. This might mean helping to re-establish working relationships or providing wellbeing support.

Always follow up any decisions or next steps in writing to the employee. Remember, grievances should be treated confidentially unless it has been agreed with the employee that they can or should be shared with others (such as for investigation).

While the good practice described in this chapter applies to all forms of employee complaints, some types of complaints might be especially difficult to manage. This may be because of the type of issue raised, because there are difficulties in establishing facts or evidence, or because of the people involved in the issue.

Common challenges in managing grievances

LACK OF CLEAR EVIDENCE

There can sometimes be conflicting evidence, or not enough evidence to make a clear decision. This is especially true when grievances are raised about another person. One person (such as the employee raising the grievance) provides a perspective, and the other offers a different one. The person hearing the grievance is faced with a difficulty – they must either decide which account they think is most likely or which they believe, or they must determine that there is insufficient evidence to proceed or make a finding. The latter situation is particularly challenging as there might be no resolution for either party.

If this arises, the grievance hearing manager should take every possible step to get evidence within the investigation. After this is exhausted, they should consider some of the following:

- Credibility of the witnesses and plausibility of accounts.
- Consistency in accounts given over time (if relevant).
- Any motivation that might be behind the particular accounts.

Then they should determine if they can make a decision. If they cannot, this should be communicated to the parties and the situation monitored in the future.

PERSONALITY CLASHES

Sometimes conflict at work results from two individuals who need to work together but have difficulty in doing so, often referred to as a personality clash. It is important, however, to establish that this is what is going on, and there is no evidence of inappropriate behaviour such as bullying. If it is genuinely that two people struggle to communicate with one another, mediation is a good option for resolution. It may not necessarily mean that these two individuals will suddenly become friends, but they may be able to find a way to work effectively together.

EMOTIONAL REACTIONS AND ESCALATIONS

It is not unusual for grievances to become emotionally charged. Raising a grievance can be difficult and stressful, and people might have strong views about the issue that they have raised. As an HR professional, if you are managing a grievance and there are strong emotions on display, strike a balance between letting people say what they need to and ensuring the situation does not escalate in a way that becomes problematic for the individual or the process. Acknowledging feelings and taking time out of meetings are simple solutions to manage this situation.

MALICIOUS COMPLAINTS

This is fairly uncommon, but it does happen. Employees can bring grievances for all sorts of reasons that are not necessarily appropriate ones. They might want to delay a disciplinary hearing, it is part of resistance to change (a topic we return to in Chapter 7), or maybe they somehow hope to gain personally from raising a grievance. Many grievance policies note that if a grievance is found to be malicious, it might amount to a disciplinary matter – check whether your organization's policy has any similar provision. If you are handling a grievance and you are concerned it might be malicious, talk to the employee about their motivations for bringing the matter to your attention. Ultimately, it is difficult to confirm that a grievance is malicious; you may need to make a decision based on what evidence you have.

RESISTANCE FROM MANAGERS

Sometimes, managers may not want to hear a grievance. They may think that a complaint is minor or misconceived, or they may feel that the employee is being difficult. They may also be concerned about hearing a grievance, as it can be complex. As an HR professional, your role in these circumstances is to advise and guide the manager. Explain the importance of fully considering grievances and the potential risks to the organization of not doing so. If they have concerns about the process, help them understand it and how they will be supported by you.

GRIEVANCES AGAINST SENIOR MANAGERS

Hearing grievances against senior managers presents a significant challenge for several reasons. Employees may be reluctant to raise concerns about senior managers, as they may fear the impact on their careers or feel sceptical about whether action would be taken. Finding an independent manager to hear the grievance can be a practical difficulty, as ideally, you would not want a more junior manager conducting the investigation. Power dynamics are also at play here, with senior managers having more power than others in the process because of their position. However, such concerns must still be investigated – senior managers are not immune to wrongdoing. If a grievance is raised about a senior manager, you could consider bringing in an external investigator – some firms offer this specialist support. Ideally, it would be supported by a senior HR professional if you have one. Think carefully about who is best placed to handle the investigation and how confidentiality will be maintained.

Employment Tribunals

When conflict is not addressed properly, or to an employee's satisfaction, they may seek to raise the matter outside of the organization through legal channels (if there are any). HR professionals are typically involved in the process of managing these claims.

In the UK, Employment Tribunals make decisions in disputes relating to employment law. They hear claims on issues such as dismissal, discrimination, harassment or equal pay. Other jurisdictions also have specialist courts to deal with employment-related claims. Each has their own rules and processes that must be adhered to which change from time to time. You may find it helpful to review the rules around employment claims, including key processes and requirements.

From an organization's perspective, it is better to avoid legal claims, although this will not always be possible. Legal claims are expensive, time-consuming and can cause reputational damage. If you receive a claim on behalf of your organization, act promptly as there will often be timescales to adhere to. Take legal advice where necessary.

> **TIP**
>
> Employment Tribunals are generally open to the public and take place in most cities. Consider attending a tribunal hearing for a few hours to familiarize yourself with what happens there. This will help you to contextualize some of the discussions in this book and advise managers where necessary. Alternatively, solicitors or HR consultancies sometimes run mock employment tribunal events. These can also provide you with an insight into how these tribunals work and how they reach decisions.

Collective conflict

Collective conflict arises when a group of employees is in conflict with the wider organization. Examples of collective conflict might include:

- disputes over pay or terms and conditions of employment
- complaints about working conditions or ways of working
- disagreement with planned organizational change, such as redundancy or new technologies

- collective legal claims – sometimes called 'class actions', where several employees bring the same claim against their employer

Collective disputes are often, but not always, raised through employee representative organizations such as trade unions (discussed in Chapter 2). If collective conflicts cannot be resolved, some might result in industrial action.

> **Industrial action:** Action taken by employees against their employer, often as a result of a workplace dispute that has not been resolved.

There are many forms of industrial action. It is usually regulated by employment legislation and requires employees and their representatives to adhere to strict procedures if the action is to be legitimate and protected. Employees are usually protected from consequences or retribution if they are taking formal, organized industrial action. One common form of industrial action is a strike.

> **Strike:** An organized stoppage of work, usually for a specific period of time, typically arranged by a trade union.

Strikes can be continuous or short term. Taking strike action aims to put pressure on the organization to meet the demands of employees. Before a strike or other form of action can take place, employees (usually trade union members) are balloted to see if they are in favour of taking action. If sufficient employees agree, according to the levels set out by legislation, the trade union must then provide notice to the employer. The strike is only considered 'official' once all the rules are complied with. If the rules are not complied with, then the action is considered unofficial, and the employer might be able to prevent it from taking place or seek compensation.

TIP

The legislation relating to industrial action, strikes and ballot varies from country to country and is subject to change from time to time. Occasionally, there are additional rules that relate to specific industries and jobs. Do some research and check what the current rules are wherever you are based. Check if any specific regulations apply to your industry or the type of workers that you employ.

Strikes are not the only form of collective industrial action that employees can take. Employees may also refuse to engage in some forms of work, such as refusing to work any overtime, or undertaking what is often called a 'work to rule'. This occurs when employees refuse to undertake any duties that are not detailed in their job description. These are sometimes known as 'actions short of a strike'.

Resolving collective conflict

Just like with individual dispute resolution, there are various ways to approach resolving collective conflict. Industrial action is often a last resort – employers do not want it for obvious reasons, and often employees do not either, not least because they are unlikely to be paid while on strike.

Some organizations might try what is known as 'collective conciliation' to address disputes with their employees. Often, this involves working with a specialist provider such as Acas, which has trained, experienced and impartial conciliators to help the parties find a solution that everyone can agree to.

Just like individual mediation, collective conciliation usually begins with the conciliator having informal discussions with the organization and employee representatives, followed by joint meetings and discussions.

Preventing collective conflict

Collective conflict can be very damaging to an organization. It can result in decreased productivity, low employee morale and engagement and financial costs. When conflict is prolonged or not properly managed, daily operations may be disrupted and the stability of organization could even be at risk. Some disputes can also attract media attention or customer complaints, further affecting reputation and customer satisfaction or retention.

Collective conflict can be avoided or minimized by creating a positive organizational culture, effective leadership and management and good HR practices. The risk of conflict can also be reduced by building effective relationships with employee representatives, as discussed in Chapter 2. Organizations (and their leaders) need to be proactive, not just reactive, when conflict arises. We will discuss strategies to avoid conflict in Chapter 8; HR professionals at all levels can support these goals.

CHAPTER SUMMARY

- Conflict of some kind in workplaces is inevitable. Not everyone will always agree or get along. Sometimes, organizations will make decisions with which employees disagree. Effective management of conflict is part of employee relations.

- Conflict can arise at an individual level, where a single employee has a complaint (known as a grievance). It may also take place at collective level where complaints or concerns arise from a group of workers.

- Collective conflict can result in forms of organized, official action by employees, such as strikes or work stoppages.

- How conflict is managed or resolved is often governed by employment legislation. Some conflict may also result in legal claims against an employer that need to be heard in a court or tribunal.

- Managing conflict is an important skill for HR professionals and people managers. Early HR professionals often support managers with individual conflicts such as grievances or complaints.

- Organizations can take proactive steps to reduce the risk of conflict, developing employee relations strategies and good HR practices that will support the employee experience.

REVIEW QUESTIONS

1 Identify three different forms of conflict that may occur at work.

2 Explain the difference between the unitary and pluralist views of conflict at work.

3 Summarize the main steps that employers should follow when an employee grievance is raised.

4 Explain the purpose of mediation and identify when it is a suitable form of dispute resolution.

Further reading

Acas, Acas Code of Practice on disciplinary and grievance procedures, https://www.acas.org.uk/acas-code-of-practice-on-disciplinary-and-grievance-procedures/html (archived at https://perma.cc/L3AV-QALY)

Keddy, J and Johnson, C (2010) *Managing Conflict at Work*, Kogan Page

Liddle, D (2023) *Managing Conflict: A practical guide to resolution in the workplace*, 2nd ed, Kogan Page

Saundry, R, Fisher, V and Kinsey, S (2019) *Managing Workplace Conflict: The changing role of HR*, Acas

Saundry, R and Unwin, P (2021) Estimating the costs of workplace conflict, Acas

Endnote

1 Saundry, R et al (2024) Managing conflict at work – policy, procedure and informal resolution, Acas, https://www.acas.org.uk/research-and-commentary/workplace-conflict/managing-conflict-at-work/report#5.-implementing-formal-procedure (archived at https://perma.cc/92Z3-43YQ)

CHAPTER FOUR

Managing employee performance

Introduction

This chapter begins with a discussion about what we mean when we talk about performance management. For some, the term is associated with a problem with performance, but as we shall see, performance management includes supporting performance too, using a variety of HR processes.

We look at the different terminology used in the field of performance management and distinguish between the various forms. Critically, we look at the work of HR professionals within performance management, discussing how they can help managers to ensure effective performance from their teams. Finally, this chapter considers the challenges that can arise when employees do not perform at work, and how these should be approached and managed.

LEARNING OBJECTIVES

By the end of this chapter, you will be able to:

- Define performance management, distinguishing between capability and conduct and the role of HR and managers.
- Summarize the evidence on performance management.

- Explain the key activities involved in effectively managing performance, including goal setting and giving effective feedback.
- Articulate how to address underperformance at work, including some key principles to follow and what to do when performance doesn't improve.

Managing performance

> **Performance management:** The activities and processes, usually undertaken by managers, of managing the performance of employees and teams.

There are two broad elements to managing performance at work:

1 Setting, maintaining and measuring standards of performance, supporting employees to meet relevant standards, and enabling them to perform at their best. This is typically achieved through activities such as performance appraisal, learning and development and reward and recognition.

2 Addressing, through appropriate processes, any problems that arise concerning performance, helping employees to improve and meet the necessary standards. This is sometimes referred to as 'capability'.

Both of these elements are usually guided by organizational policies and procedures, and sometimes by employment law. From time to time, there can be a crossover between performance and conduct, so it is important to distinguish between the two, especially because they are often dealt with separately from a policy perspective.

Capability: An employee's skills, knowledge and ability to perform their job effectively.

Conduct: Relates to an employee's behaviour at work, and their adherence to workplace rules and policies.

WHAT WOULD YOU DO?
Number 3

A manager discusses the following situation with you. Over the past four months, one of their team members has been failing to meet deadlines and making frequent errors in their work, despite receiving additional training and support. At the same time, while he gets on well with the rest of the team, the individual has shown a pattern of inappropriate behaviour. They have been dismissive about feedback and ignored instructions from the manager.

- Do you think that this is an issue of capability, or conduct?

- Explain your decision.

- What advice would you give to the manager if this situation occurred in your own organization? Use your own internal policies to guide you if you have them.

Effective approaches to performance management should be aligned with other HR activities – especially talent management.

Talent management: The combined processes that relate to attracting, recruiting, engaging, rewarding and retaining talent valuable to an organization. Performance management is one part of talent management.

Whether we are talking about performance management in terms of developing individuals or addressing performance concerns, talent management and performance management processes should be mutually supporting. The performance management process can help you to identify who has valuable talent, skills or experience in the organization. It can then help you to further develop that talent for the future.

We will now explore the two different elements of managing performance, beginning with a consideration of the roles of HR and managers in these processes.

The role of HR in managing performance

Although this varies between organizations, the role of the HR professional in performance management is to undertake some of the following:

- Provide advice on the organization's policies and any relevant employment laws, ensuring compliance with both.
- Ensure that processes are followed fairly and consistently.
- Coach and guide people managers in managing performance – this might include preparing for meetings, developing objectives or suggesting possible solutions to challenges.
- Provide practical support to people managers in managing any issues relating to performance.
- Own or oversee any systems and processes for performance management. This may also include producing reports or statistics to inform organizational decision-making.
- Train managers in the skills necessary for effective performance management.

HR is often the department that develops the systems, processes and policies that managers use to enable performance management to take place. These systems and processes must be fit for purpose, aligned to the needs of the organization and those managers, and, wherever possible, designed in partnership.

The HR role can be contrasted with the manager's role. The manager should normally take overall responsibility for managing performance and any related issues, utilizing the advice and support of HR partners and processes.

The role of managers in managing performance

Just like with HR, the manager's role in managing performance varies depending on the organization's policies, processes and systems. Generally, the manager's role in performance management includes some or all of the following:

- Supporting new starters to become effective team members.
- Setting goals and objectives, and communicating performance expectations.
- Providing ongoing feedback about progress and performance.
- Undertaking any formal performance management processes, such as appraisals or one-to-ones.
- Identifying learning and training needs and helping to facilitate development.
- Having career conversations.
- Addressing issues relating to underperformance, using the relevant processes.
- Providing reward and recognition in line with organizational approaches.

In some organizations, managers may also be involved in broader talent management or engagement initiatives.

Skills for performance management

Skilled managers can help employees perform at their best. This benefits both the employee and the organization. The CIPD states that the following skills are necessary to manage performance effectively:

- Communication.
- Listening.

- Feedback.
- Coaching.
- Emotional intelligence.[1]

Managing performance is not always an easy task. HR can play a key role in supporting managers to develop these skills through learning and development opportunities. Managers may benefit from training on setting objectives, having difficult conversations, providing effective and actionable feedback and managing underperformance.

TIP

Check what training your organization offers for its people managers on different aspects of performance management. Does it provide training on all of the aspects of performance management, and all of the necessary skills listed above? Can you identify any gaps?

The evidence for performance management

Research into performance management has established the following:

- Performance management is most effective when it is an on-going process and feedback is regular – it will be less effective if it is an occasional process (such as a once-a-year meeting).
- Feedback on performance can help people to improve, but the quality of feedback matters. If poorly handled, feedback can have no effect at all or even make performance worse.
- Performance appraisals can be subject to bias, even if managers undertaking them are not aware of this. Managers might rate people differently for all sorts of reasons, and are influenced by factors including whether they have similar personality types, or even whether the manager hired the person they are reviewing.

- Goals are important for performance management, but they need to be well-designed and properly applied.
- Employee reaction to performance reviews and feedback can differ depending on whether they feel it is useful and fair. If an employee feels that a performance review process or feedback is unfair, they may become demotivated or reject the feedback.[2]

STOP AND THINK

Why might a once-a-year meeting to discuss performance not be very effective? List any potential problems that might arise. Think about it from the perspectives of the employee, the manager and the organization.

The activities of performance management

As we've touched on, performance management encompasses a range of different activities, some of which are typically the responsibility of people managers, and some of which are the responsibility of HR professionals. Activities range from setting objectives, providing feedback, formal processes such as appraisals, identifying and supporting learning and development needs, and addressing underperformance (capability).

At an organization level, there are many reasons to have effective performance management processes. Good performance management:

- supports organizational performance through capable, skilled employees
- helps to increase employee engagement by providing scope for progression and development, as well as reward and recognition
- identifies high performers who can be further developed for the future – as well as underperformance that needs to be addressed

- provides focus, aligning the work of individuals with the broader goals of the organization

Performance management processes

Most organizations have formal policies and processes for performance management. They may also have systems to record information. These vary between organizations, and may depend on culture, resources and management capability. As we've covered, HR is often responsible for managing these systems and processes.

Processes usually include an appraisal or performance review and may also include other elements. Career conversations, formal development planning, probationary meetings (for new starters) or requirements for one-to-one meetings may all form part of the wider process of performance management.

APPRAISALS

> **Appraisal:** A formal (and usually documented) meeting between an employee and an employer in which performance is reviewed and sometimes rated. Also known as a performance review.

You have probably had an appraisal of some sort at some point in your career. Appraisals vary significantly between organizations and can range from very formal to fairly informal. Some are online and others are paper-based. Some organizations have formal policies (often developed by HR) setting out just what needs to be done and when, and others devolve these decisions to managers. Some require a rating of performance and some don't, and some also link performance to pay, whereas others keep these two things very separate. These decisions can be influenced by the kind of organization and its overall philosophy on people management. Despite their differences, most appraisals will involve the following (some of which we will then look at in more detail):

- Looking back at recent performance.
- Providing feedback to the employee about their performance – this may include a rating or performance score.
- Looking to the future and setting goals or objectives.
- Discussing any learning, support or development needs.
- Keeping a record of the conversation.

Both managers and employees are likely to need to prepare before an appraisal meeting. Managers usually collate their views and might also seek those of others who know about the employee's performance.

TIP

If you are unfamiliar with your organization's approach to performance appraisal, review their policies, guidance or documented processes, if they have any. Early career HR professionals can be asked to provide advice and guidance on performance appraisal or support the overall process of ensuring reviews are completed on time and effectively.

Sometimes, appraisal processes are criticized by employees and managers. Criticisms can include:

- Processes are too time-consuming.
- There is too much paperwork to complete, or online systems are not user-friendly.
- The system is too bureaucratic, or it is too inflexible.
- The process doesn't add any value.

If your appraisal system is receiving criticism, it is important to understand why as the complaints might be valid. Over time, systems and processes can become too detailed or detached from what the organization wants and needs. Alternatively, such criticisms may mean something else entirely – such as the manager or the employee just really does not enjoy having this sort of conversation, especially if there are difficult messages to provide.

STOP AND THINK

A common criticism of performance appraisals is that they are too process-oriented and time-consuming.

- Reflect on how your organization undertakes appraisals – do you think this criticism could apply to your approach? Consider how long they take to complete and what accompanying administration is required.
- How do you think such a criticism could be addressed?

TIP

Periodically review your performance management processes, policies and systems to ensure that they remain fit for purpose and meet the needs of all stakeholders. Seek feedback from everyone who uses them. You may also want to consider talking to trade unions, if you have them, who will also have insight into the views of the employees they represent.

GOAL SETTING

Goals or objectives are an important part of any performance management approach. Goals give employees something to focus on and can be motivational too. Individual goals and objectives can also be aligned with the organization's overall strategic goals, helping employees to see where they fit into the big picture. Managers are usually responsible for setting goals, but HR can play a role in helping them to become effective at writing them well.

> **TIP**
>
> Every employee in the organization should be able to see how their work contributes to achieving the strategic goals of the organization. To make this happen in practice, the organization needs to communicate these goals. We discuss this again in Chapter 8.

You may already be familiar with the common goal-setting framework SMART. This stands for:

- Specific – the goal clearly defines what needs to be accomplished.
- Measurable – the goal includes criteria to track progress.
- Achievable – the goal is realistic given available resources.
- Relevant – the goal aligns with other needs such as the team, organization or the individual's responsibilities.
- Timebound – the goal provides a deadline.

SMART goal theory suggests that any goal needs to include these elements to be effective. When a goal is SMART, it provides focus and clarity for employees – they know exactly what needs to be done and when. SMART goals have been criticized for being too inflexible in today's world of agile work. That being said, it can be a useful framework to guide managers (especially those new to performance management) on goal setting.

> **EXAMPLE OF A SMART GOAL**
>
> By the end of the first quarter of the financial year, attend the in-house learning programme for future leaders and successfully complete the assigned tasks to prepare you for the next opportunity to take on managerial responsibilities.

SMART isn't the only way that you can set goals. Some people also like the idea of 'stretch goals'.

> **Stretch goal:** An ambitious, high-reaching objective that goes beyond standard expectations or typical goals for the role, pushing individuals to achieve high results.

SMART goals are generally ones that you can achieve relatively easily, while stretch goals might be more difficult or challenging. They encourage people to go beyond their comfort zone. Stretch goals can help build people's confidence and grow as individuals. They should, however, be used with care; if a goal is too stretching or cannot be achieved this can have a demotivational effect – the opposite of what was intended. They might also inadvertently cause stress, pressure or even risk-taking. Stretch goals can be useful, but they should be used with care.

> **STOP AND THINK**
>
> Do you have any personal SMART or stretch goals for your early HR career? What would you like to be doing in two years from now? Keep this idea in mind until you reach the Conclusion chapter of this book, where we will undertake some action planning.

When it comes to goal setting, however, it is not just how well the goal is written that matters. As the 'R' in SMART states – a goal needs to be relevant. Ideally, this should mean it is relevant to the organization's goals and objectives.

When managers set goals, they should think about the employee's role and responsibilities, the wider goals and objectives of the team and the broader objectives of the organization. Ideally, objectives should be cascaded throughout the organization from the very top. In a cascade, the senior managers would be set their goals by the CEO or directors, and would in turn use these goals to inform the goals that they set for their team members. This process would repeat through the organization, as shown in the boxed example. This is good practice – but it does not always happen that neatly, or at all!

EXAMPLE OF A CASCADED GOAL

The CEO of a utility company sets a goal to increase customer retention by 10 per cent in 12 months by providing better customer service.

- **Senior manager objectives:** Develop a training strategy for customer service advisors and cascade this to team leaders to implement by the end of the calendar year. Undertake a formal review of all customer complaints received over the last year to identify trends; reduce formal customer complaints by 20 per cent.

- **Team leader objectives:** Ensure that all customer service advisors attend customer service excellence training within one month of their start date, and all advisors receive refresher training after one year. Undertake quality audits on 25 per cent of all calls to maintain standards. Oversee complaints to ensure 75 per cent of complaints are resolved on first contact with the customer to reduce reliance on the formal complaints procedure.

- **Customer service advisor objectives:** Meet all customer service Key Performance Indicators in 95 per cent of calls handled. Identify potential customer complaints and seek to resolve these through proactive customer service; no more than 10 per cent of calls should result in a formal complaint.

When goals are effectively cascaded, everyone in the organization is in alignment. When managers break down high-level goals into actionable objectives at different levels of the organization, everyone in the organization is clear on how they contribute to its success. It can also help to create a sense of accountability and shared purpose.

FEEDBACK

> **Feedback:** Information provided to the employee, usually by their manager, about their performance at work. Feedback may be formal, such as part of a performance appraisal process, or part of informal, everyday conversations.

Effective, actionable feedback can help employees understand their strengths, improve and grow. It can also help them to identify and address areas of necessary performance improvement. Without regular and meaningful feedback, employees may struggle to recognize performance gaps or feel undervalued. Feedback is usually the job of managers, and they may need to be trained in how to deliver it effectively.

> **TIP**
>
> Feedback should not just be about problematic performance. Employees need to know what they are doing well so that they may continue to perform and even further develop upon areas of strength.

Good feedback is:

- Timely and regular. Feedback will be most useful if it is delivered close to the event.
- Specific and constructive. Feedback should include examples, based on observations wherever possible, avoiding generalizations.
- Balanced. Feedback, especially during an appraisal, should include examples of positive performance and areas for development.

Feedback does not have to take place in a performance appraisal or formal conversation. Ideally, feedback should be part of everyday conversations between employees and managers. Sometimes, managers may need to provide difficult feedback, such as about underperformance. Managers might often seek advice from HR professionals on how to structure these conversations.

WHAT WOULD YOU DO?
Number 4

A manager has some feedback to provide to a team member – the individual has frequently missed deadlines in recent months. The manager is cautious as they know the employee is going through a difficult family situation. They ask you to help them. decide how to approach the conversation.

- What would you advise them to say?
- What other advice would you offer the manager?

PROBATION

Probation: (or probation period) is a fixed duration at the beginning of a new job during which an employee's performance, conduct and suitability for the role are assessed.

Probation periods can vary in length depending on the role and the industry. Three to six months is a typical probation period. During probation, employees typically receive training, support and regular feedback to help them succeed in their new role. If performance or behaviour does not meet expectations, the employer may extend the probation to give the employee more time to meet standards (usually with some further support) or they may choose to terminate (end) employment. A shorter notice period will often apply to those on probation than to established employees.

WHAT WOULD YOU DO?

Number 5

A new employee in your customer service department has found it very difficult to get up to speed in the role. They are making mistakes that have resulted in unhappy customers. The internal IT system seems to be a particular issue; the new starter undertook the initial training provided to all employees and has had some additional training, but still cannot operate it effectively. They are also regularly late.

Would you recommend either:

- ending the probation period and terminating employment – the employee cannot perform the role properly

- giving them more time to improve and providing more support

Come up with a rationale for your decision.

RATING PERFORMANCE

Some performance management processes involve rating or 'scoring' an employee's performance. An example might be rating whether an employee has met, exceeded, or not met expectations during the review period. Ratings can be useful to HR and leaders as they allow a 'picture' of performance to be viewed across the organization. It can tell HR how many managers believe their employees are doing well, going above and beyond, or underperforming. This can then facilitate broader conversations about managing talent or providing learning and development. If the big picture shows several underperforming employees, this might provoke discussions about possible solutions.

However, ratings can be problematic too. It is easy for managers, when thinking about what rating to give someone, to focus on the most recent performance and forget about their contribution earlier in the review period. Managers may have biases that they are unaware of, but that influence their decisions. They may unconsciously favour some employees over others, or they may find it very difficult to give difficult feedback and opt to give a neutral rating rather than tell someone that they are underperforming.

TIP

Make sure that you are familiar with how your organization rates performance. Review any relevant policies or documentation and look at the different ratings descriptors and any definitions of what they mean. If your organization does not rate performance, see if you can find out why they took this decision.

As well as the practical elements of performance management, performance management processes also usually involve methods for managing underperformance – this is a critical part of all performance management approaches, and early career HR professionals often play a role in supporting managers with this sometimes-difficult task.

Managing underperformance (capability)

Underperformance occurs when an employee fails to meet the standards required of the role. This may or may not be something that is within their control. It takes many forms, from missed deadlines to frequent errors or ongoing low-quality work. It is usually different to issues of behaviour, which we discuss in Chapter 5. Some organizations refer to this issue, and the processes they use to manage it, as 'capability'.

There can be many reasons that someone underperforms, and getting to the root cause is an important element of addressing it. Underperformance can result from:

- insufficient training or support
- personal problems
- high work demands
- lack of necessary resources
- health issues
- lack of objectives or unclear expectations
- poor management
- stress
- bullying, harassment or conflict

As you can see, some of these causes are personal and relate to the employee, whereas others relate to the organization itself. From time to time, the organization might simply have recruited the wrong person, or an employee may have taken a role that they do not enjoy, and this impacts their ability to perform.

Underperformance must be addressed, ideally promptly. Without information, it is unlikely that an employee will suddenly begin to perform! How the performance needs to be addressed will depend on the situation. Sometimes, it may be appropriate to start a formal process. In other circumstances, it might be effective to have an informal chat. There is no right or wrong answer. When performance issues are mild or have only arisen recently, the informal approach might be best. Where the issues are more serious, have been going on for some time, or if the employee has been spoken to before, a more formal or documented conversation might be required.

WHAT WOULD YOU DO?
Number 6

A long-term employee appears to be struggling in their role after some new technology has been introduced. Previously, their performance was of a high standard, and the employee has had good ratings in their appraisals. The employee has been provided with training on the new technologies, but is taking too long to do their tasks when using them. The manager is concerned that they are not going to be able to maintain performance and wants to start a capability process.

- Would you advise that the manager addresses this issue formally or informally at this stage?
- Explain your rationale.

Key principles for addressing underperformance

The following key principles set out good practice when dealing with underperformance. Remember that the process of managing underperformance should also adhere to any relevant employment laws or similar requirements.

- Employees who are underperforming should be provided with detailed information, including examples wherever possible, about that underperformance. It should be clear to them where they are not meeting the standards of the role.
- Employees should also be provided with clear information, either in the form of a job description or objectives, about exactly what is required. This will help them to understand the gap between where they are and where they need to be.
- Make sure that in any meetings or discussions, the employee has time to think and reflect, and put forward their thoughts, perspectives and suggestions.
- After being advised of a need to improve, employees should be given a reasonable timeframe in which to do so. This will depend on the role and the circumstances, as well as the size of the performance gap.
- Support should be provided to help them address the performance gap. This will also vary, but could take the form of additional training or development, or other practical support.

- Detailed notes should be taken of all discussions and agreements, so that both the employee and their manager can refer to them for transparency and clarity.

WHAT WOULD YOU DO?
Number 7

A manager approaches you to talk about one of their team members who has been underperforming for the past three months. The individual concerned has missed several deadlines, submitted incomplete work, and is not contributing to any team meetings or discussions. The manager has spoken informally to the employee, but nothing has changed. She seeks your guidance on what to do next.

- What questions would you ask the manager to better understand the issue?
- What would you suggest to the manager?

Structuring the conversation

Below is an example outline for an underperformance conversation. You can tailor this according to your policies or the situation. As an early career HR professional, you might guide managers on these conversations, or you may attend meetings to support managers and take notes.

- Explain the purpose of the meeting.
- Introduce everyone and their role in the meeting.
- Highlight that notes or a recording will be taken so that everyone can have a record of what was said.
- Set out the concerns about performance, providing specific examples.
- Remind the employee of any standards that must be met. This could be through discussing the job description, going

through previous goals or objectives, or highlighting targets or Key Performance Indicators.

- Explain the gap between the current performance and the necessary performance. Tell the employee clearly what they need to do differently.
- Allow the employee to respond or share their perspectives.
- Ask the employee if they can identify any training or other support that would help them meet the required standards.
- Check if the employee has any other points they would like to make before the meeting concludes.
- Document any next steps. This might include detailing training courses or support or setting new targets or objectives that the employee needs to complete.
- Explain clearly to the employee what might happen if performance does not improve.
- Set a review date to meet again and review performance.

When performance does not improve

There are times when, despite the best efforts and intentions, an employee is unable to reach the necessary performance standards required by the role. This may result in a process to end employment, usually referred to as termination or dismissal.

TIP

Always take advice before considering ending an employment relationship. Such processes are typically covered by employment legislation, which may vary from country to country. In addition, always check internal policies and legislative requirements before acting or providing advice to managers. Where necessary, take this advice from specialist employment lawyers.

If a decision is taken to end employment, after considering any legal implications or taking advice where necessary, there are some important considerations before any dismissal can be enacted. HR professionals may need to work with the manager to plan for this conversation. Always aim to do the following:

- Before a decision is made, always undertake a final review of the situation and confirm that this is still the most appropriate course of action in the circumstances, and that there is no alternative to a dismissal.
- Recognize that this is a difficult conversation for the manager as well as the employee. This isn't something that many managers have to do often, it may even be the first time they have to take such an action. Talk to them about any support or guidance they might need.
- Ensure that any dismissal conversation, regardless of the reason, is handled sensitively and as privately as possible. Build this into any preparation, such as the timing and the location of any meeting.
- Prepare an outline script in advance. This will help ensure that any legal requirements are met and messages are properly communicated. Keep messaging concise and professional.
- Anticipate employee reactions. While it is never good to assume how someone will react, you should plan for a range of emotional reactions, including anger, shock or sadness.
- Tell the employee what will happen next. This might be as simple as confirming practicalities, such as the last date of employment or when a formal letter will follow.

We will return to the subject of dismissal in Chapter 7.

Dos and don'ts for performance management meetings

DO:

- Prepare in advance. Gather facts, examples and feedback from other relevant individuals before the meeting. Make an outline plan for the conversation before it begins.
- Be specific. Always provide details and examples, avoiding generalizations. When people know exactly what is wrong and exactly what needs to be done, they can improve.

- Listen actively. Allow the employee to share their perspectives and any challenges they are facing. Take on board what they have to say – there might be important contributing factors that you need to hear.
- Own the conversation. Sometimes managers, especially if they find the conversation difficult, would prefer not to say that they have identified the problem, presenting feedback from others or suggesting the conversation has been requested by senior management. This might mean the employee does not understand the severity of the issue.

DON'T:

- Delay the conversation. Performance rarely improves without intervention.
- Apologize. This doesn't help the employee. You can be mindful of the impact of the conversation on the individual, but you do not have to apologize for requiring people to perform their jobs.
- Be unnecessarily critical. Stick to the facts. There is no need to make it too personal – if the feedback is too harsh, the individual might shut down.

WHAT WOULD YOU DO?
Number 8

A manager tells you that one of their team members has been underperforming for a long time. They have consistently failed to meet their targets, have high absence levels and are often late for work. A customer has recently complained about their attitude. The manager wants them to be exited from the organization as quickly as possible. You check their performance review records on the HR system, and there is no mention of performance concerns in any of the documentation. The manager confirms that the performance issues have never been raised with the employee.

- What would you advise the manager to do?
- Is termination on performance grounds a suitable response to this situation? Do additional research to help you answer this question if necessary.
- What risks can you identify if there were a dismissal?

CHAPTER SUMMARY

- Performance management incorporates two strands: setting and measuring performance standards and supporting employees to meet them, and addressing capability issues when employees do not meet these standards.

- Managers are responsible for the day-to-day performance of their teams. HR professionals can support performance management by providing policies, training, systems, and, in the case of performance issues, specialist advice.

- Performance management includes appraisals, objective setting, one-to-ones, career conversations and learning and development planning.

- Skills for effective performance management include communication, listening, feedback and coaching.

- It is important to address any issues of employee underperformance promptly. Many organizations refer to this as 'capability' and have relevant policies and processes.

- When dealing with matters of capability, organizations must follow any relevant employment law, codes of practice, collective agreements or internal policies.

- Early career HR professionals may be required to support managers with managing underperformance, providing guidance on administering elements of performance review processes, and providing training and development on the skills to manage performance.

REVIEW QUESTIONS

1 Summarize the difference between capability and conduct.

2 List three principles for managing underperformance. Explain why it is important that managers and HR adhere to these principles.

3 Describe what a manager should do if an underperforming employee does not improve – and how HR can help them tackle this issue.

Further reading

Ashdown, L (2018) *Performance Management: A practical introduction*, Kogan Page

Armstrong, M (2017) *Armstrong's Handbook of Performance Management: An evidence-based guide to delivering high performance*, 6th ed, Kogan Page

CIPD (2025) People manager guide: Effective performance management, https://www.cipd.org/uk/knowledge/guides/manager-guide-effective-performance-management/ (archived at https://perma.cc/VN5S-MRXQ)

Endnotes

1 CIPD (2025) People manager guide: Effective performance management, https://www.cipd.org/uk/knowledge/guides/manager-guide-effective-performance-management/ (archived at https://perma.cc/VN5S-MRXQ)

2 CIPD (2016) Research report. Could do better? Assessing what works in performance management, https://www.cipd.org/globalassets/media/knowledge/knowledge-hub/reports/could-do-better_2016-assessing-what-works-in-performance-management_tcm18-16874.pdf (archived at https://perma.cc/S5PL-HUWQ)

CHAPTER FIVE

Managing employee conduct and behaviour

Introduction

In this chapter, we discuss how organizations should manage issues of conduct and behaviour – often referred to as discipline. How they do so can influence the relationship with the individual employee; however, such processes are, despite confidentiality, sometimes visible in some way to other employees. Their management can therefore affect the collective relationship too.

As with Chapter 4, we consider the different roles and responsibilities involved in managing conduct and behaviour, and good practices that should be followed when dealing with issues. We also take a detailed look at the processes that can ensure fairness and legal compliance when handling disciplinary matters.

LEARNING OBJECTIVES

By the end of this chapter, you will be able to:

- Give examples of poor conduct and behaviour that could result in disciplinary action at work, including gross misconduct.
- Summarize the role of HR and managers in managing conduct and behaviour.

- Explain the key steps involved in managing issues of conduct and behaviour at work, including informal and formal routes.
- Identify the main steps of undertaking fair investigations and disciplinary meetings.
- State key principles for ensuring effective management of issues of conduct or behaviour at work.
- Understand some common issues that you might encounter when managing conduct and behaviour.

Introduction to poor conduct and behaviour

In Chapter 4, we saw how performance problems are generally dealt with through performance management (or capability) processes. In contrast, matters of conduct and behaviour are typically dealt with through disciplinary procedures.

> **Disciplinary procedure/policy:** A formal process used by an organization to address employee conduct or behaviour issues that do not meet company standards.

Disciplinary policies typically set out the procedure that should be followed when an employee has potentially demonstrated inappropriate behaviour or conduct; minimum standards for these procedures are also often included in employment legislation or codes of practice. Sometimes, organizations may choose to develop a policy that goes beyond these minimum standards. Both should always be followed to ensure fairness and consistency.

> **EXERCISE**
>
> In the UK, Acas (the Advisory, Conciliation and Arbitration Service) publish a Code of Practice for managing disciplinary (conduct)

matters. Organizations must comply with this code and their internal policies should reflect it.

Search for and fully review the Code of Practice. Familiarize yourself with the key content contained within it. Alternatively, check out if there are any similar codes or requirements in your country.

There are many aspects of conduct or behaviour at work that may amount to a disciplinary matter. For example:

- Breach of policies or workplace rules.
- Health and safety breaches.
- Lateness.
- Discrimination, bullying or harassment.
- Misuse of company property or causing damage to it.
- Theft or fraud.
- Violence.
- Failure to comply with management requests.
- Bringing the company into disrepute (damaging its reputation).

This list is not exhaustive! Disciplinary policies, and occasionally employee handbooks, will include a list of behaviour or conduct that the organization might consider to be a disciplinary matter.

Absence or attendance issues are often dealt with through specific policies, as we discuss in Chapter 6, although occasionally organizations manage these through disciplinary policies too. Check how your organization approaches this particular issue.

Some behaviour or conduct might be so serious that it is considered what is often called 'gross misconduct'.

Gross misconduct: A form of employee misconduct or behaviour at work that is so serious it may result in the termination of the employment relationship.

> EXERCISE
>
> Make a list of behaviour or conduct that you think might amount to gross misconduct. Use the definition in this chapter to help you. You may also wish to check your organization's disciplinary policy to see if it lists any forms of conduct or behaviour that it considers might amount to gross misconduct.

Whether poor conduct and behaviour is serious or not, it does need to be promptly and properly addressed. It's unlikely to improve on its own without feedback and guidance – and sometimes without consequences. Poor conduct and behaviour might also result in poor work cultures, negative impacts on other employees, such as reduced engagement or job satisfaction, workplace conflict or even legal issues, if the conduct or behaviour could amount to bullying or harassment. Setting standards is the first step.

Roles in managing conduct and behaviour

The roles of HR professionals and people managers in managing conduct and behaviour are not dissimilar to those of managing performance (refer to Chapter 4). HR professionals are usually responsible for developing policies and procedures that set out how discipline will be dealt with. They often advise on managing disciplinary issues, making sure that the organization remains compliant with all relevant employment laws. They may attend disciplinary meetings to support managers, including coaching them on good practice and appropriate sanctions. As a rule, HR professionals are not (and should not be) decision makers in disciplinary matters.

People managers are typically responsible for setting and monitoring standards of conduct and behaviour. They are usually responsible, with HR support, for managing disciplinary processes, including deciding on appropriate disciplinary sanctions where applicable. Managers may also act as an independent manager in disciplinary matters, bringing an impartial view on potential poor conduct or behaviour in other teams or departments.

Setting standards of conduct and behaviour

If you are to manage conduct and behaviour, employees first need to know the standards that are expected of them. These might be included in:

- employee handbooks or codes of conduct
- policies or procedures
- job descriptions
- induction or onboarding material
- role-related training
- training courses

Employees cannot be held accountable for their actions if they are unaware of what is expected of them. Setting standards might include saying expressly, such as in a disciplinary policy, what the company might consider to be inappropriate conduct or behaviour that might result in formal processes. Clear standards reduce ambiguity and help to create a fair and consistent working environment; employees do not have to interpret what is acceptable where they work.

STOP AND THINK

How does your current organization set standards of conduct and behaviour? Could you say that all employees know what is expected of them, or what might amount to behaviour that would result in them being disciplined?

Processes for managing conduct and behaviour

When an issue about conduct or performance arises, the organization needs to decide whether a formal disciplinary process is required. These are sometimes referred to as disciplinary meetings, hearings or procedures. Such issues do not necessarily have to be dealt with formally.

> The organization is responsible for ensuring that there is a fair procedure followed in any disciplinary matter. HR can help to ensure that processes are fair and legally compliant.

Informal approach

An informal approach to an issue of conduct might simply mean bringing the matter to the attention of the employee, reminding them of any standards or policies, and advising them that the issue should not be repeated, or that improvements are required. This might be a suitable approach if the issue is relatively minor or has only happened once.

Formal approach

A formal approach to a disciplinary matter means that the organization's policy is being followed, and this usually means that some sort of warning or sanction could apply. This might be appropriate when the issue is more serious or there have been previous issues relating to conduct or behaviour.

> TIP
>
> In the UK, if an employee is required to attend a formal meeting that could result in a sanction (such as a warning) they are legally entitled to be accompanied by a work-based colleague or trade

union representative. Always be sure to notify them of this right. Check your local employment laws to confirm if there is a similar right.

HR professionals may have to advise managers on whether a matter should be dealt with formally or informally. Often, there is no single 'right' answer to this, and you will need to balance the situation carefully, taking into account the needs of the organization, the impact on other employees and the desired outcomes.

If it is decided that an issue needs to be dealt with formally, then any organizational policy must always be followed. Make sure that you have a full understanding of any requirements set out within your policy or procedure before proceeding.

WHAT WOULD YOU DO?
Number 9

A manager has approached you about how to handle a situation in their team. An employee has been accused of regularly making inappropriate jokes in the office. There is no evidence that these jokes are discriminatory, but the manager has been told that they are making people feel uncomfortable. The manager has also been told that the individual spends a lot of their time during the working day browsing shopping sites and social media platforms.

- Would you recommend that this issue be dealt with informally or formally?
- Explain your answer.

Investigations

If a formal approach is required, the beginning of such a process (typically set out in the organization's procedure) is usually a formal investigation. The purpose of an investigation is to establish, as far as possible, all of the relevant facts of the matter.

Wherever possible, investigations should be confidential. You will inevitably have to discuss it with some people, such as witnesses, but be sure to advise them to maintain confidentiality.

TIP

The purpose of an investigation is to answer a single question: Should this matter be referred to a full, formal disciplinary hearing? This is sometimes called finding that there is a 'case to answer'. It should not make any recommendations as to what should happen within that hearing, nor any sanction that might apply.

An investigation may encompass many things depending on the nature of the issue being investigated. It will often consider some of the following:

- A meeting with the employee to hear their version of events.
- Meetings with any witnesses, or the employee's manager, if they can add any relevant information.
- Review of any relevant policies, perhaps to check if standards or rules are clear.
- Checking relevant paperwork, records, emails or IT systems.
- Attendance records.

Employees should be told than an investigation is taking place. Acas recommend that employees are told why an investigation is happening, who will be carrying it out, what they will do, how long it might take and what will happen next[1].

Investigations should be independent; the person undertaking them should normally have had no involvement with the issue. Ideally, the person in charge of the investigation will have received some training on the process. Check if your organization provides training to managers.

The investigation and any subsequent formal disciplinary meeting should be conducted by different people. An investigation could decide the following:

- Nothing should happen at all as there is 'no case to answer'.
- The matter should go forward to a disciplinary meeting.
- The matter could be dealt with informally instead, as perhaps it is not sufficiently serious to warrant a formal hearing.

> **EXERCISE**
>
> Imagine that you are investigating an allegation that several employees have been stealing items from your organization. What would you include in any investigation into the facts? Make a list.

An investigation should be of good quality. In UK law, we use the word 'reasonable' to describe the required standard. Previous cases, heard in Employment Tribunals, tell us that the matter should have been investigated as far as was possible in the circumstances.

Suspension

Sometimes it might not be appropriate for an employee to remain at work while an investigation is taking place. In such cases, you could suspend the employee. This should only be done when absolutely necessary. Suspending someone does not mean that you think they are guilty of what they have been accused of. It normally happens for one of two reasons:

- A risk to the process – the investigation could be compromised in some way by the employee remaining at work.
- A risk to individuals – in the case of an allegation such as violence or discrimination, there could be a possibility that the issue continues.

Try to ensure that suspensions do not last too long. Remember that during a suspension the employee receives all of their normal pay and benefits as they remain employed by you. It is a good idea to confirm to the employee in writing that they have been suspended and why, and what will happen next.

WHAT WOULD YOU DO?
Number 10

You are investigating an allegation that several employees have been misusing company IT systems, using them to undertake gambling, which is against your organizational policy.

- Would you recommend suspension in this situation?
- Why, or why not? Explain your rationale.

It is important to note that being investigated or suspended can be a stressful experience. Procedures must be followed – but also think about the impact on the employee and their wellbeing or mental health. Signpost sources of support if you need to.

The disciplinary meeting

As already mentioned, the disciplinary meeting (or hearing) should be conducted by someone who was not involved in the investigation. Ideally, the manager conducting the hearing will be accompanied by an HR professional who can advise on process.

THE RIGHT TO BE ACCOMPANIED

If an employee is attending a formal disciplinary hearing (not an investigation unless your policy provides for it) they can be accompanied by a trade union representative or a work-based colleague. They do not have the right to bring a legal representative, friend or family member. If the work-based colleague is not appropriate, for example, they are a potential witness, you can ask the employee to choose someone else. You should be flexible about companions if the employee is vulnerable, has a disability or may find it difficult to follow the process.

TIP

Employees must be invited to a disciplinary hearing in writing. This should explain what the hearing is about and tell the employee that they are entitled to be accompanied by a work-based colleague or trade union representative. If the outcome of the disciplinary hearing could be dismissal, the employee should be notified of this possibility.

Exactly what will happen during a disciplinary hearing will depend on your organizational processes and the issue under consideration. In the next section, we consider some key principles for managing disciplinary issues. Disciplinary hearings are normally structured as follows:

- Introduce everyone present and highlighting their role in the meeting.
- Explain the reason for the disciplinary meeting – for example, you are here to discuss lateness, an allegation or a problem with behaviour.
- Summarize any evidence collated during the investigation.
- Allow the employee to respond to the evidence or allegations. They may explain their actions, suggest mitigating circumstances or provide important context.
- Ask questions of the employee.
- Allow the employee to ask questions or make a brief statement.
- An adjournment – this is an opportunity for a break during which the manager can reflect on what they have read and heard and decide on what happens next.

- Take notes so that there is a full record of the meeting to refer to in the future if necessary.

What happens next can vary. The manager may be able to return to the meeting and confirm any decision or next steps. They may want to take longer to reflect, and the employee will be notified of the outcome or decision at a later point. Occasionally, something may come to light in the discussion that means the manager needs to go away and check some facts or conduct further investigations. No decision should be made until the manager is sure they have all of the necessary information to make one.

Deciding on sanctions

> **Disciplinary sanction:** The formal outcome resulting from a disciplinary process. This is often a formal warning but can include dismissal or other penalties.

At any disciplinary meeting, a decision needs to be made about whether the organization should take some form of action against an employee. Possible sanctions depend on relevant employment laws and the organization's policy, and possibly even the employee's contract. Organizations have a variety of different ways to describe similar types of warning. Possibilities include:

- informal (sometimes called verbal) warning
- formal warning
- dismissal or termination
- a restriction, such as an inability to apply for a promotion
- the withdrawal of a benefit

Formal warnings sometimes have stages, such as a first formal warning or a final formal warning.

> **TIP**
>
> Familiarize yourself with the sanctions that your policy provides, especially before applying any sanction in a meeting.

Sanctions must be fair, proportionate and legally compliant. Consider the following factors:

- The severity of the issue. More serious offences, such as harassment or theft, may warrant stronger action, while minor infractions may be resolved with a warning.
- Any relevant mitigating factors, such as personal circumstances, workplace pressures or unclear expectations.
- The employee's response to the issue, including whether they take accountability or show willingness to improve or address the conduct or behaviour.
- How the organization has dealt with similar cases before – you are not automatically bound to follow them, but they should guide your decision. If you are going to take a different approach, be clear as to why.
- The employee's employment history. Any previous disciplinary offences and their length of service might both be considered.
- The impact of the conduct or behaviour. For example, are there any legal risks resulting from the action, has there been an impact upon colleagues, organizational reputation or created costs?

Taking into account these factors can help you reach a balanced decision. If you give someone a warning, always be sure to tell them how long that warning will stay on their record and highlight what might happen if there is a repeat of the poor conduct or behaviour.

WHAT WOULD YOU DO?
Number 11

An employee has been reported for repeatedly making inappropriate comments towards people in the office. These comments have made colleagues uncomfortable. Despite a manager having an informal conversation with them, the behaviour has continued. A formal complaint was made, and after an investigation, it was found there was a case to answer.

During the disciplinary hearing, the employee admitted their behaviour but insisted they were just joking and did not intend to offend anyone. They said their comments were 'harmless'. The disciplinary hearing manager asks for your advice on an appropriate sanction.

- What sanction would you think is appropriate in the circumstances?
- What would you take into account when making this decision? Is there anything that you would not take into account?

Dismissal

Sometimes disciplinary proceedings can result in dismissal. This can happen when the issue is so severe that it amounts to gross misconduct, and it is considered that employment cannot continue. Dismissal can also result from multiple warnings, where there have been repeated issues of poor conduct and behaviour over some time.

Before undertaking a dismissal, always be sure to check current employment legislation and take legal advice if necessary.

Before undertaking a dismissal, you should always:

- consider if there are any alternatives to dismissal
- check that you have complied with all relevant procedures and employment legislation

- assess the risks of any dismissal for the organization and confirm that these are understood

---

WHAT WOULD YOU DO?
Number 12

You are advising on a disciplinary matter. After an allegation of theft of money in the workplace, an investigation was undertaken, which found a range of evidence to suggest that the allegation was true and there was enough evidence to proceed to a disciplinary hearing. During the hearing, the employee admitted the theft and shared that he was experiencing severe financial difficulties and had made a mistake. He apologized sincerely and offered to repay the money. The manager is not sure what to do.

- Would you advise that dismissal is appropriate in these circumstances? Why, or why not?
- Do you think that the mitigating circumstances and apology should influence the sanction that is applied? Summarize your reasoning.

If an employee is dismissed, they should be provided with a letter that confirms the dismissal, their final date of employment, and states the reason for the dismissal.

If an employee is dismissed, they may be entitled to bring a legal claim against you. This does not mean that any claim will be successful, but you should always consider this when conducting disciplinary hearings, especially for those more serious issues. If there is a legal claim, your notes of meetings and decisions will be important records. Always ensure these are comprehensive and available when you need them.

Dismissals can be difficult situations and have a personal impact on those who are handling the process as well as the employee. In Chapter 7, we explore how to handle difficult situations and the importance of practicing self-care as an early career HR professional.

Appeals

If an employee is subjected to a formal sanction, such as a warning or dismissal, they have the right to appeal the decision taken. Employees can raise an appeal on several grounds. They might argue that you made the wrong decision or that the decision was too harsh. Although uncommon, they may even find new evidence that they want you to take into account.

Organizations can set out how they want to handle appeals in their policies, but they should consider the following:

· Giving the employee a timescale in which they can appeal.
· Confirming to whom an appeal should be made.
· Appointing (wherever possible) a manager to hear the appeal who has not been involved in the process so far.

> Appeals can overturn a decision entirely or reduce a sanction that was applied, replacing it with a different one. An appeal should normally never increase the sanction to a more severe one.

An appeal might consider the following:

· The fairness of the process, including whether any internal policies have been followed.
· The quality of the investigation – whether it was thorough and reasonable in the circumstances.
· The decision itself. Does it seem reasonable, consistent and fair? If the dismissal was for misconduct, did the decision maker have good grounds to believe the employee did indeed commit the misconduct?

If you have to advise on a disciplinary appeal, guide the manager to consider each of these elements before making a decision.

Key principles for managing disciplinary issues

Following some key principles when managing disciplinary issues helps to ensure fairness and consistency for the individual and contributes to a fair working environment for everyone. You will see some similarities between this list and the principles of managing underperformance, which we covered in Chapter 4.

- Before deciding to hold a disciplinary meeting, the facts of the matter should be investigated as fully as possible.
- If a disciplinary hearing is held, the matter under discussion, such as any allegations about inappropriate conduct or behaviour, should be put to the employee in full. They should always understand the issue.
- Always give the employee time to think and reflect and put forward their version of events in any discussions or meetings.
- Detailed notes should be taken of all discussions and agreements, so that both the employee and their manager can refer to them for transparency and clarity.
- If a decision is taken as a result of a disciplinary hearing, for example, issuing a warning, the employee should always have the opportunity to appeal this decision to another, independent manager.

Dos and don'ts for disciplinary hearings

If you are supporting a manager through a disciplinary process, remember these important dos and don'ts.

DO:

- Advise the manager on how similar issues have been dealt with previously – you do not necessarily have to follow the same approach, but it should inform your decision-making process.
- Ensure that an accurate record of the conversation is taken; these notes should be shared with everyone who attended afterwards.

- Clearly explain the process that will be followed at the start of the meeting and clarify that the employee understands this.
- Watch for signs that the employee is becoming emotional, upset or even angry – you can always take a short break if you need to and then reconvene.
- Take your time – the issue needs to be fully explored, and the employee needs the opportunity to put forward their version of events in full.
- Always make sure that you send any decision in writing to the employee promptly after the meeting, clearly setting out any follow-up actions or rights of appeal.

DON'T:

- Decide for the manager – this should be their responsibility. It is also important that they deliver the decision.
- Be afraid to call an adjournment if you think it's necessary. This might be to give the employee a break, for you to confer with the manager or provide some important advice.
- Make any assumptions before the meeting begins, especially about what might be said or what sanction you might apply.
- Give a disciplinary sanction (such as a warning) if you don't need to. It is fine to take no action if that is the most appropriate thing to do.
- Don't decide on the spot. Always take at least a short adjournment before communicating any outcome.

One of the best ways to learn how to handle disciplinary meetings is to learn from more experienced colleagues. Identify any opportunities within your organization to gain this knowledge. For example, see if you could attend any meetings as an observer or note taker, or review any notes after the meeting. Talk to your manager if this is helpful.

Common issues in managing conduct and behaviour

In this section, we discuss some common issues that arise in proceedings to address conduct and behaviour – most HR professionals will deal with these challenges at some point in their career! Just like with many of our 'What would you do?' exercises, there is not necessarily a right or wrong way to deal with them. The specific context and circumstances will influence your approach – always remember the importance of fairness and reasonableness when making a decision.

Challenges to the process

Employees may not always agree with how your organization chooses to handle disciplinary matters. They may not like the manager appointed to undertake an investigation or disciplinary hearing. They may want to bring people to a meeting that you do not feel should attend, or disagree with the findings or decisions that you have made. This is not unusual. However, what matters is that you have followed a fair and reasonable process and worked in line with your policies. If an employee wishes to challenge the process, hear what they have to say – after all, from time to time, mistakes can be made. However, you are not required to agree with them!

Raising grievances during disciplinary processes

One way that employees can challenge your process is to raise a grievance, related or not to the disciplinary issue, during the investigation or the disciplinary. If this happens you will need to take a considered view of the circumstances. In some situations, it will be important to stop the disciplinary process to deal with the grievance. In others, it might be appropriate to go ahead with the disciplinary hearing and run the two processes separately, at the same time. To help you make the decision, consider the following:

- Does the grievance relate directly to the disciplinary issue, or something else entirely?
- Does the grievance suggest that there is any sort of conflict of interest, such as whether the hearing manager is an appropriate person to conduct the disciplinary meeting, or are there any suggestions of potential bias?

Going off sick during disciplinary processes

If the absence is short-term, you may be able to wait until the employee returns to address any issues of conduct or behaviour. If the employee is absent for a longer period, you will need to decide if it is appropriate to continue in the employee's absence, taking medical advice if necessary. If the disciplinary process cannot wait, you can ask the employee if there are any adjustments you can make to the process to allow them to participate. For example, an employee could make representations in writing. Keep communicating with the employee, and bear in mind the importance of being fair and reasonable within your processes.

Employees who do not engage with the process

There are lots of ways that employees might refuse to engage with an investigation or disciplinary process. They may not turn up to your meetings, refuse to answer questions, or even resign when proceedings are ongoing. You will need to give employees plenty of opportunity to engage – but ultimately, if they do not, you may need to proceed without their input and make decisions with the information that you have, even if it is incomplete.

Misconduct outside of work

Sometimes, employee conduct outside of work will come to the attention of the employer. Most of the time, what employees do outside of work is their own concern. However, there may be situations where what looks to be 'outside of work' really isn't. An example could be if an employee commits a criminal offence which impacts their ability to continue to be employed. Another would be if someone is making discriminatory or offensive social media posts that are seen by colleagues. In these situations, carefully consider whether the issue has any relation to work or other people who work for the organization.

EXAMPLE OF MISCONDUCT OUTSIDE OF WORK

One of your employees is arrested for racial abuse on a night out. No colleagues are present. The court case is published in the local newspaper, both in print and online. The article identifies the individual and refers to their work at your organization. The employer may be justified in dealing with this under disciplinary procedures. This is sometimes known as 'bringing the company into disrepute'.

TIP

When dealing with the sorts of common issues discussed here, it is a good idea to advise the managers that you are supporting to keep a record of their decisions, including what they took into account and why. If the decisions are ever subject to later scrutiny, such as in an appeal process, the information will be readily available rather than relying on memory.

CHAPTER SUMMARY

- Issues relating to conduct or behaviour are wide-ranging and usually addressed through a disciplinary process.
- The most serious form of misconduct is gross misconduct – this is conduct or behaviour that is so poor or problematic that it may result in the dismissal of the employee.

- The management of conduct and behaviour (through the disciplinary process) is governed by employment legislation and local policies and codes of practice. Early career HR professionals should be sure to follow these at all times and be ready to advise people managers to do the same when needed.

- Poor conduct and behaviour can be managed formally or informally. The formal route requires an organization to follow several steps, including an investigation, disciplinary meeting and sanctions. Fairness and ensuring legal compliance are key to the management of disciplinary matters.

- Several issues may arise when managing poor conduct and behaviour from employees challenging the process, to going off sick or not engaging with the process. Always listen to what employees have to say and take appropriate action to address their concerns.

REVIEW QUESTIONS

1 Name three principles for the effective management of disciplinary matters.

2 Identify the purpose of an investigation.

3 Explain what is meant by 'gross misconduct', giving examples of some behaviour or conduct that might meet this definition.

4 Summarize the role of HR in supporting disciplinary matters, explaining what they should and shouldn't do.

Further reading

Acas (2015) Acas Code of Practice on disciplinary and grievance procedures, https://www.acas.org.uk/acas-code-of-practice-on-disciplinary-and-grievance-procedures (archived at https://perma.cc/N4JM-BNFL)

Aylott, E (2022) *Employment Law: A practical introduction*, Kogan Page

Endnote

1 Acas (2025) Investigations at work. Step 2: Preparing to investigate, https://www.acas.org.uk/investigations-for-discipline-and-grievance-step-by-step/step-2-preparing-for-an-investigation (archived at https://perma.cc/CA67-FTUN)

CHAPTER SIX

Managing absence and attendance

Introduction

In Chapter 5, we explored how to manage employee conduct and performance. Organizations often have separate processes for managing absence, although, as this chapter shows, there are some similarities with other processes in how these issues are addressed, including key principles relating to the fairness of the process.

In this chapter, we explore the practicalities of managing absence from work and how to support attendance. Similarly to Chapter 5, we consider the different roles and responsibilities in managing absence, as well as some of the actions that organizations can take to support, identify and address absence from work. We conclude by identifying how HR professionals can support employees with specific health conditions.

LEARNING OBJECTIVES

By the end of this chapter, you will be able to:

- Summarize the purpose of absence management, how it can be done and the differing roles and responsibilities of managers and HR professionals.

- Describe the different types of absence from work and the differing implications of short- and long-term absence.
- List the different ways that organizations can measure and understand absence.
- Explain how to support an employee's attendance, for example, through making adjustments and a phased return to the workplace.
- Articulate how to address poor attendance and understand some key principles of managing absence well.
- Describe how poor mental health can affect attendance and what organizations can do to help.

Introducing absence management

Absence can be planned (such as holiday or maternity leave) or unplanned. Unplanned absence is often, but not always, a result of sickness absence. It can also occur due to emergencies, bereavement or practical issues such as commuting difficulties.

Most organizations manage absence in some form. Absence is a cost to organizations, both in real terms through the payment of sick pay, and lost productivity. Excessive absence can also place strain on colleagues or disrupt or delay operations.

When we talk about managing absence, this usually includes measuring it (we explore how to do this later in the chapter), managing problematic absence, supporting employees with health conditions and developing solutions to support attendance and health. Effective absence management strikes a balance between supporting employees who are experiencing poor health and need to take time away from work and addressing absence patterns and problems.

Managing absence can be both reactive and proactive. Reactive absence management simply involves taking action after an absence has occurred. This might be at an individual level (taking an employee through a formal process because of high absence) or at a collective level, such as introducing stress risk training for managers when stress at work has been identified as a problem.

In contrast, proactive absence management aims to improve the health and wellbeing of the workforce, thereby maximizing attendance by helping to prevent illness (especially work-related illness) from occurring. This could include developing wellbeing strategies or policies, or identifying the potential for stress before it arises.

There can be many reasons for high absence rates in a particular workplace, and these may or may not be related to the job or organization itself. Some absence is unavoidable, such as when an employee is diagnosed with a serious health condition, but some is preventable. Absence is not always necessarily about health or illness. It could also be related to some of the following:

- The culture of the organization.
- The demands or volume of work.
- Poor management.
- Personal issues such as bereavement or family problems.
- Work-related injuries or accidents.
- Low morale or engagement.
- Medical appointments.
- Conflict with colleagues or poor working relationships.

Roles and responsibilities in managing absence

In Chapter 5, we explored the different roles and responsibilities in managing conduct and performance, distinguishing between the work of HR and the work of people managers. There are some similarities to the work that HR does concerning absence management.

HR PROFESSIONALS

HR professionals can support absence management through the following:

- Developing attendance and absence policies.
- Monitoring absence and identifying information on which the organization can act.
- Introducing proactive wellbeing activities or services.
- Developing and supporting people managers in their role in managing absence.
- Providing specialist advice to managers on issues relating to absence from work.
- Supporting managers with meetings when managing complex absence issues.

MANAGER

Managers are generally responsible for the practical side of absence management. Depending on the organization and its policies, that might include undertaking absence meetings with employees, supporting employees to return to work after a period of absence, and proactively supporting attendance. We discuss these different tasks later in this chapter.

Types of absence

Absence for health-related reasons is generally categorized into short-term absence, such as absences caused by minor illnesses which last a few days, and long-term absence, where an employee needs to take a longer time away from work, often due to a more serious health condition. Long-term absence is commonly defined as being over 20 days, but this can vary.

Short-term absence

Short-term absence can be especially problematic for employers. Its often-unplanned nature may mean that it impacts productivity or customer service, or colleagues. Short-term absence is often managed through policies, trigger points and return-to-work meetings – topics we explore throughout this chapter.

Long-term absence

Long-term absence may be a result of serious or ongoing health conditions. Depending on the reason for their absence, employees who have been absent for a long period may need additional support or adjustments when returning to work. When absence is due to longer-term conditions, the conversation with employees is often less focused on levels of absence (as the employee may not be able to improve their absence) and more about support.

TIP

Some organizations have their own definitions of what amounts to short- or long-term absence. Check if this applies to your organization and whether it differs from the one suggested here.

EXERCISE

Undertake some internal research in your organization.

- What are the main reasons that employees take sickness absence from work?
- Do these differ between long-term and short-term absences?

WHAT WOULD YOU DO?
Number 13

An employee who works in a physically demanding warehouse role has been on long-term sick leave following an operation. The employee's recovery has been slow, and there's uncertainty about when they might be able to return to work, or even if they can return to their previous role at all due to some ongoing complications following the operation.

The employee has kept in touch with their manager and said that they are anxious about the future. The manager wants to be supportive and help them back to work, but is also feeling under pressure as they are coming under increasing operational targets.

- What would you recommend to the manager?
- What information would you need to make an informed decision or provide good advice?
- What steps could the organization take to support the employee to return to work?

Measuring absence

Measuring absence helps organizations to identify patterns or trends, address excessive absenteeism and understand the costs associated with their absence rates.

If absence rates are unusually high, it might suggest underlying problems that need attention. Absence from work, especially patterns of absence, can indicate potential underlying issues, either with the way that work is designed, the demands of jobs or even poor management. It can also help organizations to identify how to improve the health and wellbeing of their workforce. Organizations benefit from understanding the following:

- Why do employees take absence from work? Are there any common conditions, and are the reasons for absences related to the work or workplace?
- When do employees take absence from work? Are there any trends in the data?
- How long are the absences that employees take? Is absence short-term or long-term?

Methods

There are different ways to measure and monitor absence. At an individual level, employees are often managed through targets or triggers.

ABSENCE TRIGGERS

> **Trigger point**: Usually set in an organization's absence policy, a trigger point is a set number of absences or a total number of days of absence within a period that triggers a review of the employee's overall absence from work. Also sometimes called 'review points'.

Triggers are usually set out in an absence policy. An example of a trigger would be an employee having three periods of absence in six months. Once an employee meets a trigger, a meeting is often held with them to review their absence, and objectives may be set around improving attendance.

Some companies also use a method called the Bradford Factor to monitor absence. Here, absence is turned into an overall 'score' based on a calculation of the total number of different incidences of absence and the total number of days of absence. If someone has lots of short-term absence, they will get a higher Bradford Factor than someone who has had one long-term period of absence, even if they have the same total number of days absent. This means that employees who have lots of short-term absence (the most disruptive kind) can be identified. Again, organizations usually set a target maximum score in their policies at which point some intervention on absence is undertaken.

EXERCISE

Review your organization's attendance or absence policy if it has one. Identify what standards are included about attendance. For example, are there any stated 'trigger points' that are considered unacceptable levels of absence?

At an organizational level, most businesses have some form of overall measure of absence. Some will work out absence as a percentage, others will work out total 'working days lost' (WDL). This is the total number of working days that were not worked due to health or injury. These figures can be worked out for the whole organization or can be taken down to a departmental level to identify areas of difference that might need to be investigated.

TIP

If you don't know how your current organization measures overall employee absence, see if you can find out. Can you identify your current absence percentage rate or total WDL?

TIP

The following calculation can be used to work out your overall absence percentage. You could work this out for a week, a month or a year.

Total number of days of absence in the period × 100 /
Possible total number of days in the period

Supporting attendance at work

There are many ways to support employee attendance at work. Organizations can take a broad cultural approach, seeking to improve the health and wellbeing of the workforce in general. At a more individual level, supporting attendance might mean working with employees who have been absent from work, either to assess their fitness to work (such as through occupational health), introduce adjustments to support them in attending, or manage problematic absence. We will now explore some of the options available to employers.

> **Occupational health:** A specialist function or organization that provides advice and guidance on health-related issues at work.

Return to work meetings

A return-to-work meeting (or interview) is a structured conversation between an employee and their manager after a period of absence from work. They are one of the most common tools used to manage absence from work. There are several purposes of a return-to-work meeting:

- Establish that the employee is genuinely fit to return to work.
- Identify whether any support is required to facilitate the return and help ensure that the transition back to work is a smooth one.
- Help to address any concerns that an employee may have or answer any questions after a long period of absence.
- Discuss any issues that have contributed to the absence, as well as reinforce policies regarding attendance where appropriate.
- Demonstrate that the organization values employee health and wellbeing and fosters open communication.

The meeting should take place as soon as possible after the employee returns to work – ideally before they recommence their duties. It is a good idea to take notes on the discussion.

Normally, a return-to-work interview should be conducted by the employee's manager, and HR professionals would not be involved. The exception to this might be a manager who is inexperienced and would like some help and support, where an employee is returning after a lengthy period or serious ill-health, where there is a need for a discussion about support and adjustments, or perhaps where there are ongoing concerns about absence. The 'Tip' box gives an overview of how to structure a return-to-work meeting, whether you need to attend one to support a manager or simply need to guide a manager on what to do.

TIP

How to undertake a return-to-work meeting:

- Before the meeting, check the employee's previous absence record to see if there are previous related absences or if any triggers have been met.
- Hold the meeting in an appropriate place where you cannot be overheard or interrupted.
- Take notes to record the conversation – you might have a particular form or system to help with this.
- Welcome the employee back to work.
- Check that the employee feels that they are fit to return to normal duties.
- Take any fit note that the employee needs to submit.
- Check whether or not the employee needs any support or adjustments to help them with their return to work.
- If there are any concerns about absence levels or the employee has reached any internal trigger points that require a more detailed discussion, then advise the employee of this.

- Discuss the reason for absence where appropriate. For example, if the employee has been absent due to stress, ask them whether or not this is work-related, or they want to discuss the cause.
- Follow up on any agreed actions.

Making adjustments

Adjustments to the workplace can be a way to support attendance and help people back to work after a period of absence due to ill-health. Adjustments can be minor and do not necessarily have to be expensive. Adjustments may be required by law if an employee is considered to be disabled.

> **Disability:** Under the UK Equality Act, an employee is considered to have a disability if they have a long-term health condition that adversely affects their day-to-day activities. Long term is usually considered to be 12 months or more, although some conditions are automatically considered to be disabilities, no matter how long the employee has been living with them.

There is no reason to assume that an employee who has a disability will have a higher-than-normal level of absence from work. However, they may need adjustments to support them in managing health conditions effectively. In the UK, employers have a legal duty to make reasonable adjustments in the workplace. Examples of reasonable adjustments include:

- flexible working hours
- provision of specialist equipment
- changes to the physical workspace
- adapting recruitment processes
- flexibility to attend medical treatments

Many people develop conditions during their working life that amount to disabilities. This may require them to take some time away from work, for example, such as a diagnosis of cancer. While legally we often discuss adjustments in the context of disability, they can benefit other employees too, such as those returning to work after a short-term illness.

The 'Tips' box includes some guidance if you do need to discuss adjustments with someone, either because they have disclosed a disability or have asked for some as a result of ill-health.

TIP

Discussing adjustments with employees:

1   Don't make assumptions about the individual's needs or what adjustments might be best. They know the most about their condition, so ask questions before making suggestions.

2   Remember that some health conditions fluctuate over time. Adjustments might not need to be permanent, or they might need to change as a health condition changes.

3   Ask employees how they would like their condition to be communicated, if at all. Never share information about someone's disability or health condition without their permission.

4   Recognize that some people will find talking about their health difficult or emotional, especially if they have recently been diagnosed with a medical condition. Take your time in any meeting and give them space to explain how they feel.

5   People might feel awkward about asking for adjustments, so make it clear in any discussions (such as return to work meetings) that adjustments can be discussed.

Training managers

It's a good idea to train people managers on all aspects of managing absence, including supporting attendance. Managers should be equipped to:

- understand the causes of absence from work
- have proactive conversations about health and wellbeing with their team
- have effective conversations about problematic absence and how to manage this through internal policies
- conduct quality return to work interviews and discussions about adjustments
- identify absence problems and address them

EXERCISE

Undertake some internal research in your organization. Do you provide any training or guidance to people managers on effective absence management? If yes, what does this include? See if you identify any gaps in the training provided.

Phased return

A phased return to work is a structured approach that allows employees to gradually reintegrate into their job following an extended absence, usually as a result of illness or injury, but occasionally it might also apply to other forms of leave, such as returning from maternity or paternity leave. Instead of returning to full duties immediately, the employee works reduced hours or takes on lighter responsibilities for a set period, during which they slowly build back to their normal role or working pattern. Phased returns are particularly beneficial in cases of long-term illness or after an injury. Phased return plans can be written with the support of occupational health or medical professionals.

EXERCISE

Reflect on the information in this chapter so far, including the 'Tips' box on how to conduct return-to-work meetings. Compile a list of questions that you could recommend a manager uses when undertaking a return-to-work meeting. Include a mix of closed questions, which only require a 'yes' or 'no' answer, and open questions, which allow the employee to give a more detailed and free-form response. The open questions are likely to give you greater insights into the employee's situation and feelings.

Managing poor attendance

It is important to manage poor attendance. It can help to deter future absence, ensure fairness and identify employees who need support for their health and wellbeing. As we have already seen, organizations take different approaches and policies and procedures differ too. Some poor attendance can be 'managed', meaning that the organization can take steps to improve attendance at work, especially in terms of reducing short-term or inappropriate levels of absence. Sometimes however, there is a good reason for absence from work, or the absence is outside the employee's control. We will explore some of these examples later in this chapter.

Where poor attendance does need to be managed through processes (which may be informal or formal, just like with performance or conduct management) there are some key principles to follow. Always ensure that the principles we discuss in the next section are operated in line with any of your internal policies or local employment laws.

Key principles in managing poor attendance

First, always consider whether any management of poor attendance should be informal or formal. The informal approach may be suitable when there have been just a few absences, and an employee needs to be reminded about the importance of attendance or organizational standards and trigger points. Formal absence management may be more appropriate when absence is more problematic, impacting the organization or colleagues, or where the informal approach has already been taken and no improvement has been made.

- All meetings about absence from work should be conducted confidentially and sensitively, recognizing that some employees will find talking about their health (and especially some conditions) difficult.
- Discussions about absence from work should always be documented and stored confidentially. Notes should include any agreed actions or next steps.
- Employees should be allowed to explain the reasons for their absence and highlight any challenges they may be facing, whether work-related or personal.
- Managers should provide clear information about absence policies and expectations about attendance. The employee should be made aware of any potential consequences if attendance does not improve, such as formal procedures under the absence management policy.
- Where necessary, discussions should explore any adjustments or support that could help the employee manage their attendance more effectively, such as flexible working or phased returns.
- Employees should be encouraged to share their thoughts on what might help them improve their attendance, ensuring that any proposed solutions are practical and mutually agreed upon.

Malingering

From time to time, employees may not tell the whole truth about their absence from work. They may, for example, take more absence than is necessary, or take absence when they are not unwell. It is very difficult to 'prove' whether or not an employee's short-term absences are genuine or not. It is important not to judge or make assumptions.

Instead, it is better to explore absence (and any underlying patterns) and discuss your concerns with the employee. If you have a good reason to suspect someone's absence is not genuine, you can put this to them alongside any evidence you have.

WHAT WOULD YOU DO?
Number 14

A manager approaches you for advice. A team member has been off sick for a month after a car accident due to a 'bad back' and neck pain. Another team member has seen the absent employee working out in the gym, appearing to have no issues at all when doing so. The team member took a photograph of them lifting weights. The manager wants to start a disciplinary investigation.

- What would you advise the manager?
- What concerns do you have, if any, about the proposed disciplinary investigation?
- What other options does the manager have, other than a formal process?

TIP

Most organizations have some form of absence policy or procedure which sets out the organization's approach to absence, any standards that should be met, and what might happen if an employee does not meet an acceptable standard of absence. As an HR professional, you should ensure that you fully understand your organization's absence policy and any associated processes that measure or manage absence.

Managing complex situations

From time to time, employees can be diagnosed with serious health issues. These may be short- or long-term in nature, and their prognosis may vary significantly. In some situations, employees may need to take extended time away from work to recover. In others, employees may have learnt they will be living with a condition for the rest of their lives, and they may require adjustments to help them work effectively. HR professionals may need to support both employees and people managers through these processes, providing advice and guidance on policy and relevant employment laws, as well as on any support that is available to them.

TIP

Some of the conditions discussed here may have specific protections in law, as they amount to disabilities. Always be sure to check any legal requirements before providing advice or taking action.

CANCER

A cancer diagnosis can be shocking and life-changing, and for employees facing this challenge, support from their employer is crucial. A compassionate and flexible approach can go a long way in helping employees manage their treatment and success-fully return to work when they are ready to do so.

Cancer treatments and prognosis are highly variable. Employees can also vary significantly in their response to cancer and their work. Some will want or need to take an extended period of absence. Others will wish to retain some sort of normality and continue working around treatment if they can. The employee, along with advice from their medical team, is best placed to determine what is right for them.

Cancer charities offer a range of practical advice to both employees and employers. This is a good starting point for HR professionals and managers who have an employee with a cancer diagnosis. Macmillan, a specialist cancer charity, offers the following tips if an employee in your organization is diagnosed with cancer:[1]

- Talk to them about what they need. They should drive this.
- Take advice if you need to, either from occupational health or the employee's medical team.
- Make sure they are aware of the sickness benefits they are entitled to.
- Make adjustments that can support them to continue working or return to work, if they want to.
- Ask the employee what they want their colleagues to know – if anything.
- Remind them about sources of wellbeing and mental health support if you have them.

Don't forget to check in with the employee's manager, who may be unsure how to respond to an employee with a serious illness if this is something that they have not dealt with so far in their career.

TERMINAL ILLNESS

Receiving a diagnosis of a terminal illness can be devastating for the employee, their family and colleagues. It requires a sensitive and flexible approach. The individual may have both physical and emotional challenges, as well as concerns about finances or what will happen in the future. As with some of the other situations discussed in this chapter, there is no single way to support employees in this situation. Some employees will want to continue to work after a diagnosis, others will not or will not be able to do so. Here are some things you should think about in this difficult situation:

- Talk to employees about what they want and need during this time.
- If the individual wants to continue to work, support this wherever possible. This might include a need for flexible working, a change to working hours or adjustments to the job itself.
- Ask the employee what they want, if anything, other people to know about the situation. The employee should decide whether or not colleagues are informed.
- Provide access to wellbeing support, such as employee assistance programmes or counselling, if you have them.
- Review and provide information about other relevant benefits. For example, are there any provisions within pension arrangements for ill-health early retirement or life insurance?

If the employee decides to leave because of their diagnosis, handle this process with care and respect. Thoughtful, sensitive communication is critical. Think too about the impact on colleagues, who may also be upset. They may also benefit from signposting to wellbeing support services.

Presenteeism

> **Presenteeism:** Refers to employees who attend work while unwell, and, as a result, may be unproductive. They might do this due to internal pressures to perform or not take sick leave.

From time to time, it is not just absence from work that needs to be addressed, but attendance too. By its nature, presenteeism can be hard to identify as employees are actually at work. Unless they show signs of being visibly unwell, it may be that presenteeism happens below the radar.

There can be many reasons why someone attends work while unwell, or undertakes work when they are on holiday (sometimes called leavism). It may be related to an organizational culture where it is seen as inappropriate to take time off. Employees may be concerned about job security, or they may not want to tell someone about a particular type of medical condition. Employees who attend work while unwell might make more mistakes, be less productive or could burn out.

Presenteeism is a problem for organizations. It is not just bad for individual productivity and health. On a practical level, employees who are unwell and come to work might pass that illness onto others, adding to overall employee absence and associated costs. It may also be bad for culture – presenteeism can spread and contribute to a poor organization culture.

Organizations can take steps to address presenteeism. Some examples include:

- Train managers to recognize presenteeism and have proactive conversations with employees.
- Promote a culture of wellbeing and health, including messages about the importance of taking breaks and switching off.
- Manage workloads and job demands – when workloads are too high, employees may feel that they have to come in while unwell to keep up.
- Talk to employees about work-life balance and the importance of managing boundaries – this could include training, workshops or guidance.

STOP AND THINK

Have you ever seen signs of presenteeism in your current organization, or any previous roles you have held? What signs could you see? Did the organization do anything to tackle presenteeism?

Mental health

> **Mental health:** An aspect of individual wellbeing that allows people to contribute to society, handle the day-to-day stresses of life and reach their personal potential.

It is estimated that around one in four people will experience some sort of mental health related illness each year.[2] Mental health is also the primary reason for absence from work in the UK, according to the Health and Safety Executive.[3] This includes conditions like anxiety and depression, eating disorders, bi-polar disorder or stress. Some people will find it difficult to tell their manager or their colleagues that they are experiencing poor mental health. This can be because of mental health-related stigma or because of concerns that it might affect their chances for progression or promotion.

> **Wellbeing intervention:** Actions, events or activities that organizations take to support wellbeing in the workplace.

Many organizations now take action to support good mental health in the workplace – these are often called interventions. Here are some of the common mental health interventions taken by employers:

· Manager training.
· Mental health first aid.
· Employee assistance programmes (EAP).
· Stress risk assessments.
· Awareness days and events.
· Employee training or workshops.
· Mindfulness classes or apps.

Work can contribute to mental health difficulties, especially work-related stress. For example, stress can be caused by too many work demands.

> **Stress:** An adverse reaction that people have to the pressures placed upon them.

Practical interventions, such as those in the list above, can help employees who are experiencing poor mental health. They can also help encourage people to seek help and show that the organization cares about mental health. This, in turn, can help to reduce stigma and make it 'okay' for an employee to disclose if they are unwell and need support.

While these interventions can bring positive outcomes, organizations who want to take mental health seriously and create a culture in which people can thrive will need to go beyond merely treating the symptoms of poor mental health. This is an example of proactive absence management.

In 2017, the 'Thriving at Work' report was published. This was an independent review into mental health and employers, which looked into the financial cost to the economy of poor mental health and the potential benefits that can be gained by employers of investing in mental health support. They identified several core standards which they called on employers to implement to support positive mental health at work, reduce stigma and improve attendance. These standards suggest that employers should:

- have a 'mental health at work' plan
- develop mental health awareness among their employees
- encourage conversations about mental health
- monitor employee mental health and wellbeing
- develop effective people managers
- provide good working conditions, including support for personal development and work-life balance

If an employee has been absent from work due to their mental health, it is important to keep in touch unless this has the potential to exacerbate any condition. They may need some additional support with their return to work. This is especially important if an employee has been absent as a result of work-related stress – if the cause of the stress is not addressed or managed, then future absence may occur. The UK mental health charity Mind recommends undertaking a particular type of return-to-work discussion called a Wellbeing Action Plan. This includes discussing some of the following:

· What can help the employee stay mentally healthy at work?
· Actions that a manager can take to support the employee.
· Early warning signs that the employee is finding things difficult.
· Is there anything at work that might trigger mental health symptoms?

WHAT WOULD YOU DO?
Number 15

A manager approaches you for advice. A team member has taken several periods of absence, each for a week or more, for stress. The manager isn't sure if this is work-related stress or if it relates to matters outside of work.

· What questions would you ask to understand the issue better?
· What steps would you recommend that the manager take now?
· If the employee takes further stress-related absence, what else would you recommend?

CHAPTER SUMMARY

- Managing absence can include reactive steps, such as monitoring absence and addressing poor attendance, or proactive steps, including supporting wellbeing and proactive strategies.

- Organizations should measure and monitor absence; this will help them to spot underlying issues, identify trends and manage the costs associated with absence. Understanding the causes of absence from work is a key step in reducing absence.

- There are different ways to manage absence in the workplace, including absence trigger points, return to work meetings, offering adjustments or phased returns and training managers.

- Some forms of absence, such as cancer or mental health, may require a tailored response and support.

- Poor mental health (including stress) is the most significant reason for absence in many organizations. Interventions to support mental health in the workplace can help employees to stay well.

- The role of early career HR professionals in absence management includes monitoring and measuring absence, supporting people managers to manage absence (especially problematic absence) and advising on legal and policy issues.

REVIEW QUESTIONS

1 List three actions that organizations can take to support employee mental health in the workplace.

2 Explain the difference between short- and long-term absence, and how you can calculate an absence rate.

3 Summarize the benefits of managing attendance.

4 Identify different ways to measure employee absence.

Further reading

Dale, G (2025) HR Skills: Employee engagement and wellbeing, Kogan Page

CIPD (2023) Managing a return to work after long-term absence: guidance for people professionals, https://www.cipd.org/uk/know ledge/guides/managing-return-to-work-after-long-term-absence/?_gl=1 *1sattp*_gcl_aw*R0NMLjE3Mzg5MzA5NTYuQ2owS0NRaUEtN WE5QmhDQkFSSXNBBQ3dNa0o0d1RNNTlHUDJjRzNaS1FjM043 VlUxaU56LU1zYWIySlFBWDVMaXM5b1NVRHg3Nm1VQzFaNGF BcmlJRUFMd193Y0I.*_ga*OTQ4MDA5MTQ5LjE3MjczMzYzMD U.*_ga_D9HN5GYHYY*MTczOTM3NDg3OC45Mi4xLjE3MzkzN zQ5OTEuNTYuMC4w (archived at https://perma.cc/DMB2-V8BQ)

CIPD (2024) Terminal illness: guidance for people professionals, https://www.cipd.org/uk/knowledge/guides/terminal-illness/ (archived at https://perma.cc/88BG-DUNY)

Endnotes

1 Macmillan Cancer Support (2025) Cancer information and support, https://www.macmillan.org.uk/cancer-information-and-support/ get-help/financial-and-work/employers (archived at https://perma.cc/ Z538-9H9U)

2 Mind (2025) Mental health facts and statistics, https://www.mind.org. uk/information-support/types-of-mental-health-problems/mental-health-facts-and-statistics/

3 Health and Safety Executive (2024) Working days lost in Great Britain, https://www.hse.gov.uk/statistics/dayslost.htm (archived at https://perma.cc/8C3C-2S59)

CHAPTER SEVEN

Managing difficult issues

Introduction

In this chapter, we discuss a range of what might be considered 'difficult issues'. We take a broad view of this term, looking at things that might arise as a result of organizational decisions, such as introducing change, restructuring or reducing employee numbers. Other issues discussed in this chapter might arise as a result of employee behaviour, such as discrimination, bullying or harassment. Difficult issues may be collective or individual.

All the issues discussed in this chapter can be complex, sensitive and generate high emotions. They also all fall within the remit of the HR professional. Whether an early career or seasoned HR professional, difficult workplace issues are part of the job. We therefore consider how some of these should be managed, including some general principles for good practice and how to minimize the impact on our own mental health.

LEARNING OBJECTIVES

- Identify key principles in dealing with difficult workplace issues.
- List the skills needed to support people managers through difficult workplace issues and the dos and don'ts for supporting employees.

- Explain how to manage change well and the potential impact of doing it badly.

- Identify good practice for terminating employment, especially in redundancy situations.

- Describe how to handle complaints about discrimination, bullying or harassment.

- Recognize the potential impact on the HR professional of managing difficult issues and identify steps that can mitigate this impact.

What do we mean by difficult issues?

> TIP
>
> Remember that many of the issues discussed in this chapter may be governed by employment legislation, local codes of practice, collective agreements and organizational policies. Always check these before putting the advice in this chapter into practice.

There are many difficult and complex situations that you may become involved in managing throughout a career in HR. Remember that we have already discussed one form of difficult issue in depth in Chapter 3 – conflict in the workplace.

The HR role in managing difficult issues

The issues we discuss in this chapter are varied, and many draw on HR skills that we have discussed throughout this book. HR professionals at all stages of their career may find themselves dealing with difficult issues, but their role will vary, depending mainly on the issue itself, but also potentially the type of organization, resources, and the internal and external environment. This sort of work might be reactive, responding to issues as they arise, or proactive, identifying strategies in advance where difficult issues are planned.

HR professionals may find themselves doing some of the following:

- Providing advice to employees or managers around processes, risks or solutions – ensuring legal and policy compliance.
- Training and coaching managers on their role in handling these issues.
- Acting as a subject matter expert or bringing in specialist external advice when needed.
- Signposting employees or managers to additional resources or sources of support.
- Working with managers and leaders to develop strategies to address issues.
- Collaborating with different stakeholders, including employee groups or trade unions.

Throughout any process dealing with a difficult issue, HR professionals need to maintain professionalism, role modelling empathy, credibility and integrity.

Managers will also be involved in dealing with difficult employee relations issues. They might be hearing grievances, investigating complaints, making decisions (such as whether to make redundancies or terminate an employment contract) and leading change programmes.

Key principles in managing difficult issues

There is no single way to manage any of the issues discussed in this chapter; the only truly consistent advice is that each one should be managed following any relevant legal requirements and internal policies.

There are, however, some key principles that are relevant to most of the situations set out here for you to keep in mind, should they arise:

- Comply with internal policies and all legal requirements. This will not only support employee relations but also manage risk to the organization.
- Communicate well. Whether an individual grievance or an organization-wide change programme, clear, timely and transparent communication is key. Good communication can help to manage employee concerns and maintain employee relations, even in difficult times.
- Provide clear reasons for decisions. Even when decisions are made that might not be welcomed, providing a clear rationale will help employees understand what is happening and why and also contribute to building trust.
- Provide support for affected employees. This includes employees who are personally impacted and their colleagues and managers.
- Maintain confidentiality and discretion. Conversations should be approached with sensitivity and respect, maintaining confidentiality where necessary (if you need to share information to manage the issue, do so on a strictly need-to-know basis).
- Deliver on commitments. Whether investigating a complaint, providing support to employees, or making a decision, it is important to meet deadlines or follow through on agreements to maintain trust and integrity.
- Show empathy and concern for the impact on individuals and support their wellbeing and mental health.

Supporting people managers as an HR professional

Managers are often on the frontline of communication and decision-making when dealing with difficult employee relations issues. Depending on the type of issue (for example, restructuring), they may also be personally affected by it. Even if they are not, they may have complex emotions about it or find it stressful; new or inexperienced managers might find these issues especially difficult to navigate.

HR can provide coaching on how to conduct difficult conversations, help managers understand internal policies and legal obligations, and share best practice for handling sensitive situations. On a practical level, HR can provide detailed guidance, templates and scripts to help them with employee communication. HR professionals may also find themselves providing emotional support.

When supporting managers with difficult issues, HR professionals may wish to guide managers to:

- Acknowledge their own feelings. It is normal for managers to feel stressed, frustrated or even upset. Recognizing this can help them to navigate these difficult situations.
- Manage their feelings. If the manager is finding things difficult, they should talk to their own manager or you as their HR representative. They should try and remain calm and professional, even if employees are angry or upset.
- Set some clear boundaries. Managers will need to fulfil their role in the process and provide support to employees where necessary, but this doesn't mean that they are expected to take on emotional challenges beyond their role. They cannot necessarily 'fix' every situation, nor should they try.
- Know when to seek support and take care of their wellbeing. This is just as important as supporting their team.

WHAT WOULD YOU DO?
Number 16

A manager has been asked by senior leaders to make redundancies from within their team due to reduced financial performance. The manager knows all these people personally, and often socializes with some of them outside of work. One of the team members who might be made redundant has recently purchased a new house, and another has just had a baby. The manager approaches you to say that they are finding this very difficult. They are struggling to sleep at night and do not want to decide which team members should lose their jobs.

- What advice or recommendations would you give to the manager about the process?
- What support or advice could you provide about the impact of the process on the manager?

Supporting employees through difficult issues

This can be an area of some complexity for the HR professional, especially for those early in their career. It is important to balance supporting employees and showing empathy, and not becoming too involved or falling into the trap of providing advice. Maintaining professional boundaries is crucial to ensure that the HR professional remains an objective and trusted resource rather than becoming personally entangled in individual cases.

Dos and don'ts for supporting employees

DO:

- Signpost to sources of support and information, whether internal or external. You may also find it helpful to direct employees to internal policies that provide more information about any ongoing formal processes.
- Show empathy to the situation. Empathy is the ability to understand people's feelings and emotions, and see a situation from their perspective. It doesn't mean apologizing for it.
- Stick to your role in the process. Focus on delivering your responsibilities to help bring the matter to a conclusion.
- Manage your boundaries (discussed later in this chapter).

DON'T:

- Offer advice or your opinion. This is unlikely to be helpful for the employee – they need to reach their own conclusions or make their own decisions. It could also create future problems if the employee acts upon your advice but doesn't get the result they were hoping for.
- Make promises you can't keep. HR is usually not responsible for decision-making, nor can they necessarily require the organization to take their advice. Never make a promise to an employee that cannot be guaranteed.
- Become emotionally involved. This is sometimes easy to say but hard to do. But becoming too involved in employee support can put you in a compromising position (losing your impartiality), impact your credibility and lead to burnout.

From time to time, employees might 'blame' HR for a situation. Remember, you are just doing your job. If an employee is unhappy, try not to take it personally. You may just be the face of the decision or the process to that person. If you experience this, talk to more experienced colleagues or your manager about it.

Managing change

HR professionals are often involved in managing organizational change programmes. Change is part of organizational life and can be driven by internal and external factors such as changing technology, new customer demands or economic conditions. Even though change is common, some people find it difficult. Some change, especially the sort that HR professionals become involved in, might cause uncertainty and fear.

Often, there is a people outcome relating to strategic organizational change. It could mean moving locations, changing leadership, introducing new technology or changing ways of working. Change that might have a significant impact on employees relations can include:

- restructuring
- reducing headcount (also known as redundancies, layoffs or downsizing)
- buying or selling parts of a business (mergers and acquisitions)

TIP

If you are going to be involved in a change process in any way, make sure that you fully understand the business reason for change – why is the change necessary, and what benefits is it expected to deliver? Check what outcomes the organization aims to achieve to provide a mechanism for measuring success.

Managing change well, especially from a people perspective, is essential. This includes taking into account the emotional impact of change and the different ways that people might react to the proposal. Poorly managed change might harm employee relations. At an individual level, it may reduce employee engagement, wellbeing and motivation. It could also lead to issues with employee retention. At a collective level, it could result in some of the forms of conflict we discussed in Chapter 3.

It is often said that a large percentage of change programmes fail. This, of course, depends on how we judge success and failure. The CIPD suggests the following reasons why change can fail:

- Poor communication and project management.
- Lack of visible commitment from leaders.
- A failure to address the emotional side of change and acknowledge its impact on individuals.[1]

How change is managed and communicated, influences how employees receive it. Chapter 8 considers how organizations can successfully manage change in a way that supports good employee relations.

Some change will be unwelcome regardless of how well it is managed, especially if it relates to issues like redundancy or restructuring. Employees might resist change, formally or informally. Formal resistance to change could involve the kind of collective action we discussed in Chapter 2, such as organizing against it and seeking to take industrial action. Non-compliance with rules or requests, withholding information, reducing productivity or negative talk might all be examples of informal resistance to change. At the heart of resistance is fear and uncertainty about the future, concerns about loss of status and perceptions of fairness.

STOP AND THINK

Think about a real change situation you have seen at work – it does not have to be one from your HR career, but could be a situation you were involved in as an employee.

- What did the organization do well to manage the change?
- What didn't go well with the change process?
- Think about the people involved in the change. What emotions did they demonstrate?

As an early career HR professional, you may get involved in change in several ways:

- By supporting meetings with individuals or collective groups of employees.
- By supporting the development and delivery of change communications.
- By supporting managers through the process.

HR professionals can add value to the change process by focusing on the people element of the change. They can encourage those leading and managing the change process to think through how people might think and feel about the change, and the reactions they may have. This will help to identify ways to minimize people risk and change resistance. We look at more strategies for effective change management to support employee relations in Chapter 8.

STOP AND THINK

Imagine your organization is proposing to introduce new AI-based technologies. These will result in major changes to ways of working and it is hoped they will remove inefficiencies from work processes, help the organization speed up customer response times and save costs. All employees will need to use these AI tools to do their jobs.

- What reactions might employees have to this change? Consider positive reactions and negative reactions.

- What emotions might employees display and why?

- Can you identify any reasons employees might resist this change? If yes, what could the organization do about it?

TIP

If employees have concerns about change, or you identify the potential for conflict, you might find it helpful to increase your level of employee voice and feedback within the process. It is easy to assume that employees are simply being negative or are failing to understand the need for change. Instead, try to see employee concerns as an indication that you need to look at your change process to help support employee relations.

Termination of employment

We briefly discussed dismissal in Chapter 4, when looking at managing underperformance, and in Chapter 5, when considering conduct and behaviour. Performance and conduct are just two grounds for termination of employment. Sometimes, organizations need to make difficult decisions, such as to downsize or make redundancies. There may be times when someone starts a new role, but it becomes apparent at any early stage that they are not suited or able to undertake the role properly (a subject we discussed in Chapter 4). Organizations can be bought and sold, and employees may go with them. Sadly, at some point in their career, many HR professionals must deal with the death of an employee during their service.

Not all reasons for leaving are due to an unfortunate circumstance. Someone may be retiring, or may have been employed on a short-term contract, such as maternity cover. However, any occasion that results in employment ending can be emotional for the employee and their colleagues, and this may need to be acknowledged within the process of their leaving.

Whatever the reason for ending employment, whether voluntary or not, there will almost always be a process that needs to be followed and accompanying HR administrative activity. In terms of emotional impact as well as employee relations risk, one of the most difficult issues to manage is redundancy, also known as lay-offs, downsizing or restructuring.

TIP

In some countries, termination of employment is only permitted on specific grounds – this means you cannot end someone's employment unless it is for one of a given list of permissible reasons without risk of a legal claim from the employee. In the UK, these reasons are discussed in the Employment Rights Act 1996. Always consult relevant legislation when considering dismissal.

Redundancy

> **Redundancy:** The reduction of a workforce because a particular job or role is no longer necessary.

Redundancies may result from many different reasons. It can be a response to financial difficulties, changes in technology or ways of working (meaning some roles are no longer needed), relocation of a workplace or even a complete closure of one.

> TIP
>
> Many countries have specific employment legislation which dictates how to manage employees in redundancy situations. This may involve consultation with employees and their representatives, notification requirements and time limits that must be adhered to. Failure to follow legislation could lead to employees claiming compensation. Employees are also usually entitled to some sort of redundancy or severance pay. Always check relevant employment legislation before commencing any redundancy process, taking legal advice if necessary.

In this chapter, we don't focus on specific legal requirements relating to redundancy, but instead look at good practice for supporting employees in redundancy situations. HR professionals may often be involved in the following:

- Developing communication plans, from organization-wide messaging to scripts for individual meetings.
- Supporting managers with employee meetings.
- Advising on legal and process requirements.
- Consulting with trade unions or workforce representatives.
- Administering the redundancy process, such as sending letters and making any necessary payments.

Normally, managers would be responsible for delivering communication, undertaking meetings with employees (including appeals against redundancy if there are any) and potentially deciding what roles to make redundant.

COMMUNICATING REDUNDANCIES

Communicating redundancies can be challenging, not least because any communication needs to do the following three things at once:

- Let employees know about the difficult issue sensitively and with acknowledgement of the emotional context.
- Give practical information about the next steps.
- Deliver legally required messages to stay compliant with employment legislation.

Depending on the number of redundancies, messages might be delivered in a one-to-one setting with an individual employee or to the workforce as a whole. Good practice in redundancy communications includes messages that are:

- sensitive and empathetic
- transparent, providing explanations about why decisions have been made
- clear on next steps and timescales
- straightforward, using accessible language and avoiding jargon

When employees first hear about redundancies, they may feel shocked and need time to process the information. You should always provide a contact for further questions and follow-up after the initial communication. Thoughtful, honest and humane communication can make a difficult situation more manageable for everyone involved.

STOP AND THINK

Reflect on what you have read so far on the topic of redundancy. Consider some of the following questions:

- What emotions do you think employees typically feel when they first hear they are at risk of redundancy?
- How do you anticipate employees might feel after they have had time to process the news?
- What reactions might employees have that could be difficult for you to manage?
- If you have been involved in a redundancy situation, what emotions did you observe in employees?

TIP

Senior leaders play a key role in redundancy situations. They shape how the process is perceived and should be visible and address concerns openly. It is likely that other employees, even if not personally affected by redundancies, will be anxious or uncertain. Addressing their concerns and providing reassurances (where possible) is important.

PREPARING MANAGERS TO MANAGE REDUNDANCY

HR professionals play an important role in helping managers prepare for handling redundancy situations. They can do this through training, guidance and coaching. Managers may feel anxious about delivering such messages, so HR professionals can offer guidance on how to communicate clearly and compassionately.

On a practical level, providing managers with scripts, FAQs documents, and key messaging helps ensure consistency and minimizes the risk of miscommunication. If you are supporting managers in this situation, consider some of the following:

- Provide a briefing on relevant employment legislation and company policies. If your organization recognizes trade unions, include information on their role.
- Talk to managers about the sort of emotional reactions they may face and how they can respond to them.
- Provide guidance or training on how to conduct meetings, or, if it is required by your policy or situation, the processes for selecting employees for redundancy.
- Ensure managers are aware of the different sources of support that are available for employees who may be made redundant.

SUPPORTING EMPLOYEES DURING REDUNDANCY

Wherever possible, seek to support employees who are leaving you through redundancy. This could include career transition support (sometimes called outplacement), time off for interviews for new roles, help with CVs or wellbeing and mental health support.

> **TIP**
>
> Redundancy affects employees who stay, as well as those who leave. It can result in something called 'survivor syndrome', where remaining employees experience difficult emotions, including guilt and anxiety.

After redundancies have concluded, the organization should acknowledge the emotional impact on the wider team. If communication has been effective and transparent throughout, you will have already taken steps to mitigate the impact on others. Where possible, provide reassurances about job security and the future direction of the organization, as this can help alleviate concerns. Ensure managers undertake check-ins with their team, offering them an opportunity to voice feelings and ask questions. If appropriate, you may also want to consider some simple team cohesion activities.

As an HR professional, managing redundancies, whether on a small or large scale, can be challenging. It is perhaps one of the more difficult aspects of an HR role. However, if redundancies are necessary, managing them effectively, fairly and respectfully will help to make the process as easy as it can be. HR professionals play an important role in helping employees to feel supported and respected even in the most difficult of situations. In turn, this supports the organization in maintaining future employee relations.

Discrimination, bullying and harassment

Discrimination, bullying and harassment are terms that are sometimes used interchangeably, but they do have specific meanings, some of which are set out in legislation.

> **Discrimination:** Treating someone less favourably because they have a characteristic that is protected by law, such as race, religion, sex or disability.
> This definition is based on the UK Equality Act 2010.

> **Bullying:** Repeated, harmful and unwanted behaviour directed at an employee (or group of employees).

> **Harassment:** Unwanted conduct related to a relevant protected characteristic, which has the purpose or effect of violating an individual's dignity or creating an intimidating, hostile, degrading, humiliating or offensive environment for that individual.
> This definition is based on the UK Equality Act 2010.

Behaviours that might amount to discrimination, bullying or harassment include:

- unwanted physical contact
- inappropriate language
- excessive criticism of someone's work
- isolation or exclusion
- name-calling or verbal abuse
- unfair treatment
- unwelcome advances
- threatening behaviour

Discrimination and harassment can be one-off events or happen on an ongoing basis. These behaviours can have a serious and long-term impact on employees, especially if they are left unaddressed.

Many organizations have a policy and process for raising concerns about discrimination, bullying and harassment. This might be the standard grievance procedure, such as the one we discussed in Chapter 3, or it might be a separate route just for equality issues. Some organizations even have anonymous reporting mechanisms for those who have witnessed issues of discrimination, bullying or harassment but who do not feel that they can come forward formally. The legal implications of discrimination, bullying and harassment mean that organizations should not only take cases seriously but should also adhere to any legal requirements in responding to them. A failure to address cases of discrimination, bullying and harassment might leave the employer open to legal claims from employees.

In this section, we focus on how complaints should be handled, and the role of HR professionals in this process. Note, however, that this is a reactive approach. Ideally, organizations should take proactive steps to prevent discrimination, bullying and harassment from happening in the first place. They should be clear that such behaviour will not be tolerated and, if found, will be taken seriously and addressed through disciplinary procedures. More generally, organizations need to create a supportive environment where employees feel safe to raise concerns, can be confident that their concerns will be addressed fairly, and where equality and inclusion are treated as important business priorities.

TIP

Check if your organization has a specific policy for raising concerns about discrimination, bullying and harassment. Sometimes, these polices are referred to as 'dignity or respect at work policies'. Alternatively, provisions for raising concerns might be included in a broader equality policy. Make sure that you are familiar with any reporting procedures contained within the policy, as well as any key principles.

Handling employee complaints

Employees may find it difficult to raise a complaint about discrimination, bullying or harassment, perhaps fearing retaliation or damage to their professional reputation. They may also feel that their concerns won't be taken seriously or that the process of reporting and resolving the issue will be lengthy and stressful. Power dynamics in the workplace can also contribute to this reluctance, especially if the alleged behaviour involves someone in a higher position of authority.

Any complaint of discrimination, bullying or harassment should be fully investigated. We discussed investigations in Chapter 5 in relation to misconduct. Many of the principles of investigating discrimination, bullying or harassment are similar to the ones we discussed earlier:

- Follow your internal policy if you have one.
- Have the complaint investigated by an independent manager.
- Ensure that the investigation is impartial, and the investigating manager keeps an open mind.
- Keep records of the investigation and any decisions made.

- Keep everyone involved in the investigation up to date and undertake it in a reasonable timescale.
- Investigate as far as is practicable, considering witness evidence, records, policies or documents. Exactly what will be included in the investigation will depend on the circumstances and the nature of the complaint.

The employee who has raised a complaint may need support while it is being considered under your processes. This might include formal support for wellbeing or mental health, such as an employee assistance programme, if you have one.

EXERCISE

An employee approaches you in confidence and tells you that they are being bullied by two colleagues in their team. They don't know what to do but want it to stop. Identify relevant policies within your organization. What advice should you provide to the employee, using those policies? Consider:

- What options does your policy provide concerning raising this issue?
- What sources of support does your policy provide to employees who are experiencing bullying?

EXERCISE

Reflect on the content of this chapter and your experience. Ask yourself the following questions:

- Do you have any experience with the difficult issues discussed in this chapter? If so, what skills do you think you have that helped you to resolve the issue(s), and do you have any development needs?
- Consider areas where you do not currently have experience. How does thinking about managing such issues make you feel? Do you have any concerns about managing these difficult issues?

- You are likely to have to deal with many of the difficult issues discussed here at some point in your career. How could you gain more skills, knowledge and experience in these areas, to ensure that you can be effective?

You may want to include some of your reflections in your plan for personal development (refer to the Conclusion chapter).

Managing the personal impact of difficult work

Some elements of employee relations work, such as managing conflict or dealing with difficult employee issues, can affect HR professionals. This kind of work is emotionally demanding and requires resilience. Over time, the emotional demands of managing these issues can lead to stress, fatigue, or even burnout if you do not have adequate support or self-care strategies. This can be especially true during the early stages of your career if you are experiencing these situations for the first time. Don't forget there may also be times when HR professionals are themselves impacted by programmes that they are required to deliver, such as change or restructuring.

It is important, therefore, to look after your own mental health when working in employee relations. There is no right or wrong way to do this, and what works for one person does not necessarily work for another. Here are a few ideas that can help you maintain your health and wellbeing while working in employee relations:

- Undertake regular self-care – reflect on what helps you to feel relaxed, de-stress or switch off, and build this into your routine. Don't wait until you feel stressed to act.
- When managing difficult situations, take additional steps to look after yourself. If necessary, seek advice and support from your manager or more experienced colleagues.
- Identify and set some boundaries – check out some specific ideas in the next section.

- If you identify that you are experiencing any health or wellbeing challenges as a result of the work that you are doing, seek help promptly. You are also an employee, so utilize any wellbeing or mental health support provided by your employer.

Managing boundaries

Part of self-care involves setting boundaries; these can help to protect against overwork or emotional overwhelm. A boundary is a form of personal 'rule' that helps you manage the balance between work and non-work and protect yourself from over-working. Examples of boundaries for HR work could include:

- Setting limits around working hours and availability, especially around the use of digital tools.
- Saying no to requests that are outside of the scope of your role.
- Maintaining relationship boundaries – for example, some HR professionals prefer not to attend social events outside of work to avoid the potential for conflict between professional and personal lives. Similarly, some HR professionals don't want to connect with colleagues on social media platforms.
- Placing limits on the support provided. It can be easy for HR professionals to fall into a role of providing advice or solving problems, but this may not be appropriate for the role or healthy for anyone involved.

STOP AND THINK

If possible, reflect on any work that you are currently involved in or may have undertaken in the past.

- What emotional or personal challenges could you identify in that work?
- What steps can you take in future employee relations work that would help you to manage boundaries or prevent stress?

- What can you do to manage a healthy work-life balance?

As with the previous exercise, you may want to include some of these reflections in your plan for future development in the Conclusion chapter.

CHAPTER SUMMARY

- HR and employee relations professionals may get involved in a range of complex, sensitive and difficult issues relating to their employees. These might include termination, change or bullying and harassment.

- Many of what we would call 'difficult issues' will be governed by employment legislation. HR professionals should always check relevant laws, internal policies or codes of practice before taking action.

- When dealing with difficult issues, good communication is key. Timely, regular and transparent communication, even if the message is a difficult one, will help to build trust and support long-term employee relations.

- Any complaint about discrimination, bullying or harassment should be looked into promptly, following organizational policy and process.

- Managing difficult issues can have a personal impact on HR professionals themselves – they should take steps to establish boundaries and avoid burnout.

REVIEW QUESTIONS

1 Describe the role of HR professionals in managing difficult situations.

2 Explain the importance of HR professionals taking care of themselves when managing difficult employee relations

issues. Suggest at least one practical way that they can do this.

3 Summarize key principles of effectively and fairly managing difficult employee relations issues.

4 List three steps that an HR professional can take to ensure fair and effective redundancy processes.

Further reading

Acas, Discrimination and bulling, https://www.acas.org.uk/discrimination-and-bullying (archived at https://perma.cc/7PC4-6MD9)

Cameron, E and Green, M (2019) *Making Sense of Change Management: A complete guide to the models, tools and techniques of organisational change*, 5th ed, Kogan Page

Lewis, D, Sargeant, M and Schwab, B (2023) *Employment Law: The essentials*,16th ed, Kogan Page

Endnote

1 CIPD (2024) Change management, https://www.cipd.org/uk/knowledge/factsheets/change-management-factsheet/ (archived at https://perma.cc/P45Q-8QWC)

CHAPTER EIGHT

Achieving good employee relations

Introduction

This chapter focuses primarily on the collective relationship between organizations and their employees and how this might be developed and maintained. Some of the discussions and suggestions made here align with broader areas of HR work, from HR policy to employee engagement.

We discuss the link between HR policies and practices and employee relations, and review strategies and practical actions that organizations can take if they want to develop a culture supportive of good employee relations.

LEARNING OBJECTIVES

By the end of this chapter, you will be able to:

- Explain what constitutes good employee relations for organizations, in both business-as-usual and more difficult times.

- Identify strategic and practical ways to achieve good employee relations.

- Highlight where employee relations aligns with HR activities and initiatives.

- Describe different mechanisms and methods for understanding the state of your employee relations.
- Name some ways to support good employee relations, including some quick wins and ways to maintain employee relations in difficult times.

What constitutes good employee relations?

We considered this question briefly in Chapter 1. Generally, an organization that has good employee relations has high levels of employee involvement, commitment and engagement, and low levels of individual and collective conflict. When managing difficult issues, such as underperformance, poor conduct or some of the complex issues discussed in Chapter 7, good employee relations has a slightly different context. It means handling these issues effectively, professionally and in line with employment legislation and internal policies.

In contrast, an organization that has poor employee relations may have high levels of workplace conflict (and associated costs), a lack of trust, problems with attracting and retaining employees and legal claims. There are clear business benefits from working to create good employee relations.

Employee relations strategies

Almost all organizations have a strategy setting out the overall aims or mission of the organization, even if it is not formally communicated. Strategies are typically accompanied by a series of objectives or goals that the organization seeks to achieve. Whether it is expressed (through people goals or a specific people strategy) or not, many of these goals will rest on the activities of employees within the organization.

> **TIP**
>
> Strategies are usually shared with employees. If you are unsure about yours or which key objectives have been set for the organization, do some internal research. Check if any organizational objectives relate specifically to your people.

A people (or HR) strategy is a long-term plan for people within an organization. It will typically include HR activities or programmes from how people are recruited to how talent is retained, developed and rewarded. People strategies often consider the organization's current needs, while also thinking about future workforce needs. Organizations that wish to achieve and maintain good employee relations should make this a strategic priority.

From an employee relations perspective, people strategies might also include many of the subjects we have discussed in this book, such as employee representation, participation and involvement and how the employee engagement experience is supported. They should positively impact the business and improve the way that people work.

Senior HR professionals are usually responsible for developing formal strategies in partnership with senior leaders. According to the CIPD, in addition to issues of participation and representation, some of the strategic elements of people strategies may also include:

- developing an organizational culture that supports performance and improves the way that people work
- managing employment risk and reputational issues
- establishing suitable frameworks for consultation, employee voice and negotiation, including using employee feedback to make improvements[1]

For any people or employee relations strategy to be effective, it must be aligned with the overall organizational strategy, supporting its objectives through people.

As an early career HR professional, you are unlikely to be involved in developing strategy, but you can still play an active role in supporting it. First, make sure that you understand your organization's people or employee relations strategy, if you have one. Then consider how the work you currently undertake supports those aims and objectives. Talk to your manager if you're not sure. Good HR practices at all levels enable good employee relations.

By actively engaging with the people or employee relations strategy, you may be able to identify opportunities for improvement in day-to-day HR activities. Whether it's streamlining routine HR tasks, supporting managers with their role or gathering feedback on HR initiatives, small contributions can have a meaningful impact on the broader work of the HR function.

HR practices and employee relations

Many of the typical practices and activities within HR's remit may influence relations with employees. This includes the terms and conditions of employment, such as pay and reward, but goes beyond it, looking at issues like organizational culture, employee engagement and the employee experience. We discuss some of these topics in more depth later in this chapter.

Many other activities described within this book, such as performance, absence, conduct and behaviour management and how difficult issues are managed also influence employee relations. Early career HR professionals often play a significant role in these activities when they work closely with managers to address them.

Effective HR policies and practices can support good employee relations. They can be at least partially responsible for:

- the experience of applying for a job and joining the organization, key to establishing the initial relationship
- the development of people policies that reflect good practice
- how employees are recognized and rewarded for their work, including who gets promoted
- communication with employees, from employee voice activities to managing the processes of employee feedback
- the people policies that set out how people are managed, especially when there are issues relating to performance, conduct, behaviour and health
- the effective and timely management of difficult people issues
- how change is communicated and managed
- the development and learning opportunities for employees, including how managers are developed to have the skills necessary for people and employee relations management

Many of these activities influence how people feel about their organization, tapping into core issues such as fairness, inclusion and trust, which are all part of the employment relationship and psychological contract. As a reminder, we discussed the psychological contract in Chapter 1. It describes the unwritten expectations between employees and the organization.

When some of these activities are handled poorly, not only will they not be resolved, leading to longer-term problems, but they may also contribute to poor employee relations. For example, if a performance review process is inconsistent, lacks transparency or appears biased, this may harm relations and jeopardize the psychological contract. Errors in routine HR administration can also affect the employee experience. As we discussed in Chapter 1, this can result in reduced employee well-being, more conflict and complaints, and low job satisfaction. HR professionals should therefore focus on the accuracy and effectiveness of HR processes and routine administration, ensure policies reflect good practice and consider each element of the employment experience to make it as good as it can be.

As an early career HR professional, you may not be directly responsible or involved in all the areas listed here. However, you can influence employee relations at an individual or collective level in any aspect of your HR work.

STOP AND THINK

Look at the list above of HR activities and interventions and see where your current HR role (if you have one) contributes to them. Identify how doing this HR work effectively, fairly and in line with good practice can contribute to good employee relations at your organization.

Understanding the state of your employee relations

How do your employees feel about working for your organization? As individuals, are they motivated, satisfied, healthy and engaged? Do they feel valued, understand your mission and objectives and their role in achieving these? Collectively, how would employee representatives describe your organization and how people think and feel about working there?

There are many different ways to understand employee relations. The employee engagement survey is one of the most commonly used methods. This tends to focus on how 'engaged' an employee is, a definition that is generally considered to incorporate how people think and feel about their organization and the extent to which they are satisfied, energized and committed. Surveys often translate some of these ideas into percentages, but also provide scope for employees to share their thoughts and feelings in their own words.

Trade unions, or other employee groups, are also key data sources for organizations. They have insight into the issues affecting their members, including areas that some might feel that they could not raise through other employee voice channels.

Further insight into the state of employee relations can be gained from exit interviews, turnover data, sickness absence data and through monitoring and analysing information on the types of complaints, grievances or legal claims made against the organization. If you want to learn more about specific issues, you could consider focus groups or pulse surveys that ask targeted questions. These are all forms of employee voice, which we will discuss more later in this chapter.

STOP AND THINK

How are your employee relations at your organization? Are there any formal or informal mechanisms to understand the state of your employment relationships? If so, see if you can access these to inform your understanding of your organization. If not, think about your informal sources. What do they tell you about the state of your employee relations?

Understanding more about how employees view the relationship is also linked to the psychological contract, which includes how employees expect to be treated, and what they believe they will receive in return for their work. This is wider than simply the wage they are paid, but ideas about how secure their job will be, what sort of development opportunities they might be able to access and how fairly they will be treated. Fairness and trust are key to the psychological contract.

STOP AND THINK

Think about your current or a previous organization, whether you are currently working as an HR professional or not.

- Would you describe it as a 'fair' organization?
- What does this word mean to you in an employment context?
- What does an 'unfair' organization look like or do?

Leaders, managers and HR professionals, through their policies and practices, all influence the psychological contract, just like they influence employee engagement and employee relations.

Whatever term you choose to use: engagement, relations, or psychological contract, listening to your employees and finding out more about how they feel is a good idea.

When you understand your current state of employee relations, you can determine where improvement is needed. Through your measurement and understanding process, you might also gain insight into how employee relations can be improved. Your understanding might inform future people strategies (as we have already discussed) or practical plans for improving employee relations.

Improving employee relations

Employee relations can be improved not only through HR practices but also through integrated, planned activities and interventions. These may be incorporated into the sort of formal employee relations strategies that we discussed earlier in this chapter. We will now discuss some ways that organizations can positively influence the relationships between them and the people that work for them. Many of these will have a long-term focus, although we will conclude with some quick-win ideas too that can support longer-term plans.

Employee Voice

Employee voice is an enabler of employee engagement.[2] This means that it can help organizations to engage their employees, which in turn brings benefits for the organization. We defined employee voice in Chapter 1 as an umbrella term for different ways that employees provide feedback, contribute their perspectives and influence those things that affect their working lives. Voice can be collective (often conducted through trade unions) or individual – the perspectives of a single employee.

Voice is more than just listening; it is also acting on feedback. For this section, we will consider voice widely, including employee involvement and participation.

Put very simply, employees want to have a dialogue with their employer. Many organizations have a range of different ways to 'hear' the employee voice – we discussed some of these earlier in the chapter when considering the ways that you can assess the state of employee relations where you work.

EXERCISE

Undertake some internal research to identify which methods your organization uses to hear the employee voice. Consider both formal and informal methods.

- How does your organization share or use the feedback or information provided by employees?

- Do you think your organization has a good approach to employee voice? See if you can identify any areas for improvement.

There is a crossover between ideas about employee voice and those about participation and involvement. As we discussed in Chapter 2, involvement and participation goes further than mechanisms for listening and taking feedback, incorporating communication from the organization to employees and active employee involvement with decision making. Often, this includes a collective consultation element with trade unions.

TIP

Even if a trade union is not recognized, remember that there is a legal requirement to consult employees for some people activity, such as redundancies or employee transfers. Make sure you are familiar with legal requirements wherever you work.

Engaging with employees, listening to their ideas and feedback and involving them in decisions will help to support an environment with good employee relations. Organizations that want to maximize the benefits of voice, involvement and participation may wish to consider undertaking a measurement and understanding exercise as described earlier in this chapter. Other suggestions for maximizing the benefits include:

- Set up internal groups to provide feedback on working for the organization from their unique perspectives. For example, connecting with working parents, disabled employees, or employees with particular characteristics will provide new insight for HR and leaders.
- Provide training for managers on issues relating to voice and involving employees in local and team decision-making.
- Establish employee advisory groups that can work with the organization on particular issues. For example, some trade unions will elect health and safety representatives – this approach can promote joint problem solving and improve efficiency.
- Consider introducing reverse mentoring or back-to-the-floor initiatives where senior managers can spend time working with more junior employees to build relationships and open new communication flows.
- Set up a mechanism to demonstrate to employees how the organization has acted upon feedback, suggestions and ideas received. This is sometimes referred to as 'you said, we did' and lets employees know their feedback is valued.

EXERCISE

Review the list above and identify if any of these suggestions could suit your organization and fit with your people strategy. If you think one of them could result in benefits or improvements,

identify how you could take this forward. Who would need to
approve the proposal, and what resources would you need?
Outline a plan.

Internal communication

Internal communication is linked to employee voice and can
have a huge impact on employee relations. Employees want to
be informed; they also need information if they are to meaning-
fully participate in activities like collective bargaining.

> **Internal communication:** All communications, whether formal or
> informal, that take place within an organization. Often, but not
> necessarily, from leaders to employees.

Many large organizations have an internal communications
function; this should be aligned with people and employee
relations strategies. In smaller organizations, internal communications might be the role of managers and leaders.
Sometimes, internal communication is part of HR, but even
when it isn't, much of what needs to be communicated within
an organization needs HR input. Depending on the organization, there might be a formal strategy or set of objectives for
internal communication.

In the next section, we cover employee engagement.
Employees need information about the strategic direction of the
organization if we want to ensure their engagement and commitment. Communication can take many forms:

- Blogs, vlogs or updates from senior leaders.
- Employee handbooks, policies or guidance.
- Staff intranets or internal social media platforms.
- Strategic plans.
- Newsletters or emails.

- Tools like Microsoft Teams or Slack.
- Meetings – online or in person.
- Posters, notice boards or leaflets.
- Dedicated employee communication apps.
- Townhall-style events.

Good communication is mutually supportive of many of the discussions in this chapter. It supports voice, enables engagement, helps organizational change succeed and is part of the management of any difficult employee relations issue. Crucially, it helps everyone, including employees and their representatives, to understand the direction of the organization, promoting meaning and shared purpose. Good communication is a shared responsibility between leaders, managers and specialist teams. When leaders are great communicators, it also helps to build trust.

Effective communication depends on the technologies an organization uses, the kind of work people do, how dispersed people are and industry norms. Good communication is:

- regular
- open and transparent (wherever possible)
- consistent

Good communication will also use a mix of methods to meet the different communication needs of employees. For example, using both traditional and digital media, and both asynchronous (where messages are sent and received at different times, such as email) and synchronous (real-time communication, such as video conferencing) tools.

STOP AND THINK

Reflect on the communications that take place in your organization:

- Who has responsibility for internal communications?

- How do you update employees on business performance, progress against objectives or new plans?
- What methods of communication do you use?
- Overall, do you have good internal communication or is there room for improvement?

If you want to ensure that internal communication supports employee relations:

- Train managers in the importance of good communication and how to communicate well. This will help them to play a role in cascading messages and keeping their team informed.
- Ensure that effective communication is part of any leadership development activity. Senior leaders set the tone for communication across the whole organization and they must have highly developed skills.
- For any organizational change or difficult employee relations issues, have a formal communication plan as part of the overall strategy and approach. As part of this plan, think about the emotions people might experience and the information they need to know.
- Review the different communication needs of employees. These might be influenced by the type of work they do or where they work, or other factors like cultural norms or language in a global organization. Ensure your mix of communication meets these different needs.
- Think about the purpose of the communication. Do you want to simply provide information, or do you want the recipient to do something as a result? If so, there should be a 'call to action' in the communication, clearly telling people what to do next.
- If you recognize a trade union, involve them in communication plans and strategies. They can play a valuable role in sharing and translating messages to employees.

As an early career HR professional, you may not be able to influence all internal communications within your organization. However, you may be able to influence or support communications that relate to HR activity. Identify any opportunities you may have to be part of communicating with your employees.

Employee engagement

As we have seen, employee engagement is about how committed, enthusiastic and satisfied people are with their work and organization. There are good business reasons to care about employee engagement. Engaged employees are less likely to leave or take sickness absence, and they are often more motivated and productive.

There has been a great deal of research into employee engagement and what drives it. Not all of it agrees, however! Some potential learnings from this research might influence how we think about employee relations, for example, the importance of employee voice.

Some organizations and HR professionals use the term 'employee engagement' to describe similar ideas to employee relations, although they are a little different. Engagement is a more modern term; the history of the term 'employee relations' means that some people still associate it mainly with organizations that recognize trade unions.

Engagement is a psychological state, while employee relations describes the relationship between the employer and employee, but there is a crossover between the ideas and what drives them. Improving engagement in an evidence-based way is likely to also improve the broader relationships and the collective dimension of employee relations.

According to the research organization Engage for Success, employee engagement can also be supported by having a clear strategic narrative (direction) for the business, along with good managers and organizational integrity.[3] This means that the values of the organization are clear and well-practised. Promises are kept, information is shared, and people are consistent with their behaviour and expectations. Other research into employee engagement highlights the importance of having a caring manager, good relationships with colleagues, opportunities for development and the ability to be able to use your personal strengths at work.[4] All of these individual elements can also help to create a positive working environment and influence the everyday relationship between employees and the organization.

EXERCISE

Review the research referred to in this discussion on engagement, using the endnotes to help you, taking particular notice of the drivers and enablers of engagement that they identify. You could complement this with additional reading on employee engagement. Identify any drivers or enablers of engagement that your organization is not maximizing to improve overall employee engagement. How could these be improved?

Developing managers for good employee relations

As we have seen in our discussions on managing performance, conduct and difficult issues, some of the activities that fall under the umbrella of employee relations can be challenging. There are legal issues and risks to consider, and some of the conversations will no doubt be difficult for some managers, especially those who are new to managerial work. There are emotional aspects to deal with too. Managers can benefit from specific training and guidance on aspects of employee relations. Some of the skills that managers will need to successfully support good employee relations are those that are part of general good management, such as good communication, active listening and providing meaningful feedback. General skills around performance management will also support good employee relations. Other more specific training could include:

- an overview on key employment legislation relevant to managing people
- addressing and resolving conflict
- having difficult conversations
- theoretical perspectives from research on what supports good employee relations – and why this matters
- handling complaints and undertaking investigations

STOP AND THINK

You may find it helpful to research and reflect on the managers at your organization, and their skills, knowledge and behaviour for managing employee relations.

- What current or previous formal management development has been provided to people managers, and how were employee relations addressed within it?

- How effectively do managers manage performance, conduct, behaviour and attendance? Is formal training on your policies available?

- Do you believe that managers understand the potential impact of their day-to-day behaviour, style and activity on employee relations? From your own experiences or observations, where do you see areas for improvement?

- Are there any barriers preventing managers in your organization from effectively supporting good employee relations?

Use the answers to these questions to consider how, as an early career HR professional, you can help managers to develop the skills and behaviours that they need to support engagement and wellbeing.

Effective management of change

In Chapter 7, we explored the challenges of managing change and the impact that poorly managing it can have on employee relations. Change does not necessarily have to be a difficult issue. You can help to ensure that it does not become one by considering some of the following:

- Have a clear rationale for change that is explained to employees. This should address why the change is necessary or why any particular decisions have been taken.
- Continue with regular communication – information gaps can create uncertainty. Use multiple channels of communication to ensure you reach everyone.
- Provide a role for employee feedback so that employees feel they have a voice in the process.
- Provide training to the managers involved in the change – they should be able to articulate effective change management processes and the importance of employee feelings in successful change.
- Set some clear, measurable objectives for the change activity, and track progress against them.
- Ensure senior leaders are visible in the change process to champion the change. It may be helpful to appoint an overall sponsor or champion for the change activity.
- Share successes and quick wins as the change activity continues.

TIP

There are several popular organizational change models. These are approaches or frameworks that help to successfully manage the process of change. Well-known change models include Kotter's 8-Step Change Model, ADKAR and Lewin's Freeze/ Unfreeze model. Familiarize yourself with these models and what they contain. Understanding change from a theoretical perspective will help you provide relevant and helpful advice to people managers involved in change activities.

When supporting change as an early career HR professional, keep in mind the key principles for managing difficult issues, discussed in Chapter 7. These can also add to the potential for change success and reduce the potential for a negative impact on employee relations.

Organizational culture

We defined organizational culture in Chapter 1 as 'how things are done around here'. This includes the values, norms and accepted ways of working in any particular organization. Organizations can have strong cultures or weak ones. In this context, a strong culture is one where employees understand the core values and purpose of the organization. These are embedded into ways of working. In contrast, a weak culture is one where there is a lack of consistency of behaviour, values are non-existent or are not taken into account in decision making. There might be a lack of clarity about what is acceptable.

We can also think about organizational cultures as being 'good' or healthy – or the opposite where cultures are problematic or even toxic. It has often been said that culture is more important than strategy. In other words, even if you have a brilliant strategy, if you do not have a positive culture and people who are engaged with it, the strategy may fail. The CIPD describes a positive organizational culture as one where employees understand the organization and feel that their employee voice matters.[5] It also highlights the importance of meaning at work, inclusion, values and employee behaviour in creating an organizational climate in which employees would wish to work.

Organizational culture is shaped over time as a result of many different actions, activities, behaviours and decisions. It also comes from the stories people tell and the history of the organization. HR policies and practices can influence it too, in terms of what behaviour is rewarded, how managers are developed and employees are engaged. Culture can therefore be difficult to influence, especially in the short term.

In many respects, culture is a culmination of many of the things discussed so far in this chapter – employee voice, developing managers, effective change management, employee involvement and great human resources practices. If you take proactive steps on these issues, and handle individual employee relations issues well, this will contribute to a good culture.

HR professionals who want to help their organization develop a culture that enables good employee relations should think about which aspects discussed in this chapter need attention. Although culture does generally need a long-term approach, quick wins can be helpful too. They can send signals about what matters and support the more strategic activities discussed in this chapter.

Ten quick wins for employee relations

Quick wins can help to create a positive employee experience and good relationships between employees and the organization. As you will see, some of these quick wins are aligned with common HR practices or activities.

1 Recognize employees. From a traditional 'employee of the month' scheme to local team recognition, make sure that good work is seen and valued.
2 Make leaders visible and accessible. Leaders who are available and approachable will be able to build trust and foster a connection with employees.
3 Brief employees on the organization regularly. 'Townhall' style events, blogs or video messages can all be utilized to help keep employees up to date with what is happening in the organization, especially progress against strategic goals.

4 Implement suggestion schemes. These might seem a little old-fashioned, but employees often have ideas that they don't know how to raise. Provide a way for them to suggest ideas or provide feedback.

5 Support wellbeing. Wellbeing activities send a signal to employees that their health matters. They support attendance and reduce the risk of work-related stress and burnout.

6 Promote equality, diversity and inclusion. Employees value working for an inclusive organization. It goes to the heart of feelings of fairness, which is key to good employee relations.

7 Celebrate employee milestones and anniversaries. These are simple but valued methods for recognition.

8 Encourage work-life balance. Showing respect for employee's lives outside of work, and offering relevant flexibility, also helps to signal an employer who cares about their people.

9 Provide development opportunities. Learning and growth are motivators, and they support employee engagement and wellbeing. Employees value the opportunity to learn and develop.

10 Set up social activities. Although these are not for everyone, many employees enjoy the relationships that they make at work. Support these but make them voluntary.

On their own, few of these suggestions will make a significant difference to employee relations. But together they can help create a positive work environment in which employees feel valued, cared for and included.

STOP AND THINK

Reflect on the quick-win ideas in this section and identify if there are any that you could suggest taking forward in your organization.

Maintaining employee relations in difficult times

In Chapter 7, we explored several difficult issues that can arise in employee relations, both individual and collective.

Organizations and their leaders want good employee relations. As we have discussed, organizations occasionally need to take actions that are potentially damaging to relationships, such as restructuring or change, weighing up the risk of doing so against other business imperatives. Wherever possible, involve employees and their representatives, informing and consulting.

The principles for managing difficult issues set out in Chapter 7 can help you with maintaining relationships during such circumstances. Combine those with some of the suggestions here for improving employee relations; together, these can help your organization to weather the storm and maintain a strong relationship with the people that work for you.

CHAPTER SUMMARY

- 'Good' employee relations means having involved and engaged employees and low levels of individual and collective conflict, as well as handling difficult issues fairly, consistently and in line with legislation and organizational policies.

- An organization can take a planned, strategic approach to managing and positively influencing its relationship with employees.

- HR practices, especially those that influence the employee experience, can also positively influence employee relations when these are effectively delivered.

- The overall culture of the organization also influences the broader relationship between employees and the organization.

- Employee voice, training managers and effective change management can all support good employee relations.

- Organizations may find it useful to measure employee sentiment and feelings about their work and organization. This can help to identify problem areas for employee relations.

REVIEW QUESTIONS

1 Define employee voice and explain how it can positively support employee relations.

2 Name three actions that employers can take to improve employee relations.

3 Explain how HR practices and activities can support good employee relations.

Further reading

Cowan, D (2017) *Strategic Internal Communication: How to build employee engagement and performance*, 2nd ed, Kogan Page
Dale, G (2025) *HR Skills: Employee engagement and wellbeing*, Kogan Page
Whitter, B (2023) *Employee Experience Strategy*, Kogan Page

Endnotes

1 CIPD (2025) The Profession Map, https://www.cipd.org/uk/the-people-profession/the-profession-map/explore-the-profession-map/specialist-knowledge/employee-relations/ (archived at https://perma.cc/4SJX-QME2)

2 Engage for Success. Employee Voice, https://engageforsuccess.org/employee-voice/ (archived at https://perma.cc/YL6J-YP9B)

3 Engage for Success. The Four Enablers, https://engageforsuccess.org/the-four-enablers/ (archived at https://perma.cc/Z29Y-EN73)

4 Gallup. What Is Employee Engagement and How Do You Improve It?, https://www.gallup.com/workplace/285674/improve-employee-engagement-workplace.aspx#ite-357473 (archived at https://perma.cc/KW96-U6FJ)

5 CIPD (2025) CIPD Viewpoints, https://www.cipd.org/en/views-and-insights/cipd-viewpoint/organisational-culture/ (archived at https://perma.cc/43HN-2JUX)

Conclusion

This book has sought to introduce individual and collective employee relations to the early career HR professional. The concluding chapter provides further guidance on developing your skills, knowledge, competencies and behaviours to support your future in this important area of HR work.

As you work through this chapter, reflect on your current skills, keeping in mind your own organization's culture and desired future career direction.

Remember that as a discipline, HR is always developing, and new research often emerges. Along with the ever-changing context of work, HR professionals must keep up to date and evolve their approach to remain effective partners to managers and the broader organization.

LEARNING OBJECTIVES

By the end of this chapter, you will be able to:

- Review and reflect on your skills in the area of employee relations.

- Summarize how the changing world of work might influence employee relations.

- Identify areas for future learning.

- Develop an action plan for continuous professional development.

Reviewing your knowledge, skills and behaviour

As we discussed in Chapter 1, the world of work is always changing. Organizations respond to changes in their environment, whether that's customer demands, new technologies or economic and political change. This, in turn, influences the relationship between employers and employees. Organizations and HR professionals need to develop new approaches to employee relations in response to this constant change.

As an early career HR professional, you must constantly develop your skills and knowledge in employee relations. The 'review questions' at the end of each chapter can help you assess your understanding of the subjects discussed throughout this book. To assess your current skills and knowledge further, you may find it useful to undertake the skills and knowledge assessment exercise in the box. As you do this, revisit the discussions of HR skills throughout this book, particularly in Chapter 1, where we discussed skills necessary for employee relations, and other chapters, where we discussed skills needed to manage issues such as absence, conflict or discipline.

KNOWLEDGE, SKILLS AND BEHAVIOUR ASSESSMENT – EMPLOYEE RELATIONS

Ask yourself the following questions.

Knowledge

- To what extent are you aware of current trends, research and good practice in employee relations and associated ideas?

- Can you summarize the factors, either within or outside of work, that affect employee relations positively or negatively?

- Do you fully understand any policies within your organization on subjects related to the management of absence, conduct and performance? Can you also identify relevant employment laws that relate to these subjects?

- Do you understand when to apply informal resolutions versus formal policies?
- Can you explain the benefits of your strategic approaches to employee relations to employees and managers?

Skills

- Do you feel confident guiding managers and employees through grievance and disciplinary processes?
- Can you assess and advise on employee relations-related risks?
- How well do you manage your own emotions when dealing with difficult situations?
- Are you an effective communicator and relationship builder?
- Do you approach every employee relations situation with an open mind, avoiding assumptions or biases?
- Are you considered trusted and credible by the managers in your organization?
- Can you work effectively with a range of stakeholders, balancing their different needs?

Behaviour

- How do you ensure you behave ethically in your HR work, especially when dealing with difficult, sensitive or confidential matters?
- How do you ensure that you continually develop as an HR professional?
- How do you ensure inclusivity and fairness in your employee relations work?
- Do you proactively manage employee relations rather than just react to issues as they arise?

TIP

Below are five top tips to help you continue your learning and development in employee relations. Follow these to maximize your potential for future success. Remember that the world of work is always changing. These changes may create new employee relations challenges that need to be addressed, whether we are talking about managing difficult situations or improving the relationship between organizations and the people that work for them.

1 Keep up to date with developments in employment law. It does not stand still!

2 Stay informed about industry best practice. Just like employment law, ideas around good practice, especially in related areas like employee experience and engagement, also refresh from time to time.

3 Continue to develop your theoretical knowledge of employee relations. This will help you make good, evidence-based decisions and advise your organization effectively. It will also help to build your credibility as a professional.

4 Seek out a mentor or opportunities for peer-to-peer learning. Many employee relations skills can be best developed through undertaking them or watching more experienced colleagues.

5 Attend relevant training or professional development courses. Look out for training and learning that will support your ongoing development.

Action planning for continuous professional development

This book has offered opportunities for reflection, practical tips, exercises and recommendations to share. The final step is to reflect on what you have read, think about your career goals and ambitions (bearing in mind your current skills, knowledge and experience) and combine these into a plan for your continuing professional development (CPD).

CPD allows you to plan for your future learning and development, taking into account experiences, skills, knowledge and behaviour, with the ultimate aim of developing your professional HR practice. Everyone's plan will be different, reflecting their unique situation, experiences to date, opportunities and goals. While the focus is on how to build your skills in employee relations, consider your wider HR practice too, as no HR topic is truly independent of another. As this book has demonstrated, the different elements of HR work align, interconnect and overlap. Consider concepts such as employee engagement and motivation, the employee experience of working for an organization, and organizational culture.

Personal SWOT analysis

You may well have heard of a SWOT analysis or undertaken one during your academic studies. A personal SWOT analysis is a valuable tool for early-career HR professionals to reflect on their strengths, weaknesses, opportunities, and threats in relation to their skills, experience, capabilities and knowledge. Undertaking a self-assessment exercise can help you to reflect, identifying what you are already good at, but also areas that need further development to progress your career as an HR professional.

The SWOT analysis process is simple. Begin by listing your strengths; what skills, knowledge and experience do you already have concerning employee relations, and the different aspects of it discussed in this book. Think about both the individual and collective elements of employee relations. In the next section, we look at translating the personal SWOT analysis into a plan – this can include not just working on your development areas but further maximizing existing areas of strength.

The second step is to reflect on your weaknesses, or areas for development in employee relations. These might include areas where you have less practical experience or theoretical knowledge, less confidence or where you feel that you can learn more.

Next, consider the opportunities that are available to you. This might include some ideas from the section on the future of work, or they might be more specific to your organization or role. Consider workplace trends, opportunities for informal learning or formal training or any other chances that might exist (or that you can create!) to further advance your skills, experience and knowledge.

Finally, look at potential threats. These might be external factors, such as changes in the political, social, technological or economic landscape. They might be internal too, within your organization, or personal, such as a particular trait that you are aware of. Is there anything that might get in the way of you developing your competency in the field of employee relations?

After you have completed the exercise, use your reflections and ideas to create an action plan that will help you to continue to develop your HR career. Where you have identified areas for development, think about how you might tackle these. Where you have identified threats, how can you ensure that they do not derail your future professional development?

Action plan

Creating an action plan for continuous learning can help provide structure and clarity to your learning and personal development. It can help you identify goals, set timelines, and break down what you want to learn into discreet, manageable steps. You can then easily track your progress.

Use your self-assessment reflections to help you, along with any of the other reflections you have undertaken as you have worked through this book. Use the template provided to set yourself some learning goals in relation to your further development in employee relations. Aim to set yourself at least three objectives that can help to further your skills, knowledge or experience. Provide as much detail as possible when drafting your action plan and the specific goals within it. Table 9.1 shows an action plan with the two rows completed as examples.

TABLE 9.1 An action plan for continuous learning

What is your specific objective?	How will achieving this objective support your HR career or ambitions?	By when will you achieve this goal?	How will you know when you have been successful?	What resources do you need to achieve your objective?
Gain experience of undertaking grievance meetings by acting as a note taker for senior HR colleagues.	I will be able improve the advice and support I provide to managers.	By the end of the year.	I will be able to undertake meetings independently.	Support from senior HR colleagues, effective notetaking skills.
Build a working knowledge of redundancy legislation, including employer obligations and employee rights.	I will be able to advise on and manage this difficult employee relations issue if it arises.	Within three months.	I will be able to explain redundancy legislation and provide advice on the topic if required to do so.	Online resources from government websites. Guidance from professional bodies.

Answers to 'What would you do?' exercises

This appendix gives some suggested responses or approaches for the 'What would you do?' exercises included in this book. Each of these answers are based on current UK legislation, relevant codes of practice and good employment practice. They are indicative only; you may decide that in your particular organizational context, a different approach would be more suited or supportive of your employee relations strategy.

WHAT WOULD YOU DO? NUMBER 1

This could be a matter for mediation, but some potential problems should be considered first. There is a power imbalance as the manager has more seniority than the employee. The issues that the manager has raised could be matters for performance management, especially if the employee is not delivering work on time. If a manager is behaving appropriately and reasonably in setting deadlines and following up work, this would not usually amount to bullying behaviour. So before recommending mediation, more information is required. A good starting point would be to talk more to the manager about whether they can provide any examples or evidence regarding the issues they have discussed with you.

WHAT WOULD YOU DO? NUMBER 2

The issues should be investigated, following the organization's grievance procedure. The senior manager may or may not be the most suitable person to do this – consider if they are sufficiently independent or if they would need to input into the grievance in any way. The grievance process should begin by meeting with the employee and establishing as much detail as possible, including their evidence. This would normally be followed by notifying the manager about whom the complaint has been made, and then meeting with them to hear their point of view and discuss any other relevant information. There may be a need to undertake further investigation, such as talking to potential witnesses, depending on the discussions that take place. If it is established that the manager has treated the employee unfairly or unreasonably, action may need to be taken. This will depend on the findings of the investigation.

WHAT WOULD YOU DO? NUMBER 3

This could be both capability *and* conduct. However, it is always a good idea to explore any connections between the two. For example, is the employee's inappropriate behaviour somehow related to their underperformance, such as an anxiety response to knowing their manager is concerned about their errors? There are different ways that this situation could be addressed. The manager could treat these two things separately and commence formal proceedings. Alternatively, they could opt for a single, documented conversation during which all concerns are set out, clear objectives for improvement communicated, and information provided about what next steps might follow if the employee does not improve both their behaviour and their performance.

WHAT WOULD YOU DO? NUMBER 4

The manager should have a conversation with the employee to highlight the missed deadlines and any impact this has had on the team, other colleagues or associated work. If this is the first time the employee has missed deadlines, then this could be handled informally initially. The manager can be empathetic towards the employee's personal issues, but this is not a reason not to begin the conversation. The employee needs to know there is an issue that they need to address. The manager can ask the employee if there is any reason behind the missed deadlines and check if the employee needs any support to help them improve – being open-minded to any suggestions. Depending on the conversation, it may be appropriate for the manager to highlight the potential of future, more formal processes if improvements are made. It is important to check that the employee understands what is required of them regarding work deadlines.

WHAT WOULD YOU DO? NUMBER 5

The organization may be able to terminate employment if local legislation permits it. However, as they have already invested in recruitment and training costs, it may be worth continuing to support the employee, at least for a little while, to reach the required standards. There may, of course, come a time when the organization concludes the employee is unable to reach the required standards, or the time investment required to help them is too great – this is a judgement call as well as a legal one. It may also be relevant to factor in the impact that this individual's non-performance is having on the rest of the team or any team objectives.

It would be a good idea to have a documented conversation with the employee to explore any problems that might be getting in the way of them reaching the standard, including any support they might need. It would also be good practice to check that the employee is aware of the standards required.

The employee's lateness is a separate issue from their performance – they should be spoken to about this too, and reminded of the requirement to attend work on time. The consequences of the performance issues should also be raised with the employee, including the impact on customers. If this approach does not yield results, termination during the probation period might be appropriate.

WHAT WOULD YOU DO? NUMBER 6

As this employee has a good performance record and is long-serving, an informal approach to begin with may be useful here. The employee may be aware of the problems – they might even be feeling awkward about their challenges with the new technologies or fearful of the consequences. Capability proceedings might be appropriate at some point – deciding when to do this is a judgement call. Before starting such formal proceedings, explore any additional support that they might require, beginning with a conversation with them. Remember that conversations of this nature should always be documented as they may be important in any future formal processes.

WHAT WOULD YOU DO? NUMBER 7

First, find out more about what was said in the previous informal conversations. Were any deadlines or objectives set, and did the manager provide any deadlines for improvement? Did the manager take any notes or document the conversation so that there is a record of what was said?

As an informal conversation has taken place already and no improvement has been made, this might indicate it is time for a more formal process.

WHAT WOULD YOU DO? NUMBER 8

There appear to be two issues here: performance issues and absence and lateness. In relation to the absence, it is important to identify if any ongoing or long-term health issues might be relevant to any approaches or decisions made. The fact that underperformance has been allowed to continue for some time is potentially problematic. It may be appropriate to talk to the manager about why this has happened, and the importance of making sure these conversations take place in the future to avoid this situation occurring. It would not usually be good practice to terminate someone for performance when the problem has not been previously brought to their attention. This could compromise the fairness of any dismissal.

A conversation should begin with the employee as soon as possible to discuss the absence and lateness, and the performance. This should include information on the outcome of the performance issue – the customer complaint. The discussion should be documented, and the employee advised about improvements that need to be made, deadlines for these improvements and information on the potential of future formal proceedings if improvements are not made. Where necessary, follow up on any health concerns, such as with occupational health.

WHAT WOULD YOU DO? NUMBER 9

Although different, both of the issues here (inappropriate comments in the office and potential misuse of IT systems) are related to conduct and behaviour. They would both usually therefore be dealt with through a disciplinary policy or procedure.

The inappropriate comments could present risk to the organization even if they are not discriminatory, as they are making other employees feel uncomfortable. Not addressing this could create a toxic work environment and lead other employees to conclude that poor behaviour is acceptable or not addressed by the organization.

Similarly, the employee may be wasting time at work, impacting their own productivity and possibly that of the team.

Whether this is managed formally or informally is a judgment call, and the manager may have some important insight here. If an informal approach is taken, then very clear standards of conduct and behaviour should be set; it would be acceptable to say that both of these issues need to cease with immediate effect, as they do not require the employee to learn to improve. Whether formal or informal, conversations should be documented. Remember – some employees may be more upset by some of the comments than they are letting on, as not everyone will feel confident enough to raise a grievance. When coming to a decision, consider any organizational risks that might apply.

WHAT WOULD YOU DO? NUMBER 10

Before deciding whether to suspend, consider if there are any risks to the investigation or other employees if those under investigation stay working while it is ongoing. This might depend on the nature of their role; could they, for example, interfere with any of the evidence or attempt to influence any witnesses? How serious do you think the issue is? For example, has there been any organization impact, risk or loss? If you do decide to suspend during the investigation, follow the guidance in this book on managing suspensions.

WHAT WOULD YOU DO? NUMBER 11

The individual's intent when making jokes or comments is not relevant. It is not a defence to say that the intention was harmless or fun – what matters is how the jokes or comments affect the individual who hears them. This is, however, quite a common 'defence' to such allegations.

The nature of the jokes or comments is relevant. Are they discriminatory? Could they amount to bullying or harassment? This might indicate that a more severe punishment is appropriate.

Remember that, as well as being inappropriate in the workplace, such behaviour can create risk to the organization too, such as grievances from other employees. Consider whether your policies, training and induction processes make it clear that such behaviour is not permitted. Similarly, check whether the employee has ever done anything like this in the past, or how any other similar cases have been approached, if there have been any.

While outside of the immediate disciplinary matter, it may also indicate that a general refresher across the organization would be helpful to prevent such issues from arising in the future.

WHAT WOULD YOU DO? NUMBER 12

Issues relating to theft go to the heart of the employment relationship. For many organizations, they will result in dismissal, as the trust between the employee and the organization is fundamentally damaged. It is, however, not essential that such an issue results in dismissal. It would be up to the organization (usually through the disciplinary hearing manager) to determine whether the mitigating circumstances or the apology are sufficient to give a less severe sanction. Individuals make mistakes, and you may decide to treat this as a one-off error. If you decide to dismiss, consider any risks relating to the dismissal carefully, and follow all employment legislation and relevant policies.

WHAT WOULD YOU DO? NUMBER 13

This would be a good example of when formal medical or occupational health should be sought before making a decision. This may help to answer the questions about the impact of the health condition on future employment. It may also identify opportunities to help the employee return to work – for example, could any amended duties be suitable, or could a phased or part-time return be an option? Could any specialist equipment help the employee to return?

Remember that if an employee has a long-term health condition, this might need to be treated as a disability, requiring reasonable adjustments to be considered or made.

Once advice has been sought, a conversation should begin with the employee to explore options for the future.

WHAT WOULD YOU DO? NUMBER 14

This issue should be approached with caution. When an employee is off sick, there are no restrictions on what they can do in their time. In this situation, the employee could be taking exercise on the advice of a doctor or to help with symptoms. It is important not to jump to the conclusion that they are engaged in inappropriate behaviour or are not unwell. Managers should also be cautious about using evidence such as a photograph taken by another employee.

If there are concerns that an employee is not genuinely ill while taking time off work for ill-health, investigate them but do it sensitively. A good start would be involving occupational health or taking medical advice on the condition, potential options to support a return to work and the possible length of the absence. The manager could also arrange to have a keeping in touch conversation with the employee to ascertain their current situation.

WHAT WOULD YOU DO? NUMBER 15

Before providing advice, it would be useful to understand if the manager has had any conversations with the employee so far. Have any return-to-work meetings taken place, and what was discussed? It would also be helpful to learn more about the work that the employee is involved in, and if there is anything happening that might be contributing to work-related stress.

The next steps should be to talk to the employee – this could be through a return-to-work interview or an informal discussion. It is important to understand the cause of the stress, and in particular if it is due to a work-related issue that might need to be addressed. Are there any factors in the employee's job role, such as particular demands, that could be a cause of stress? A referral to occupational health can also provide information about how to reduce stress. The employee can also be signposted to any internal wellbeing services that you have available.

Ultimately, it might be necessary to manage the ongoing absence through any internal absence management policies.

WHAT WOULD YOU DO? NUMBER 16

The manager may have to make the decisions about redundancies, as they will have the most relevant information on employees. That decision, however, could be supported or ratified by HR or other management if that is appropriate.

In this situation, it is important to reassure the manager, acknowledging the impact on them. They may also need to be signposted to sources of wellbeing support to help them through the process. The manager should be advised to discount any information that they have on personal circumstances and focus on any relevant information or selection criteria when making any decisions. They can also be supported by HR in preparing for and conducting any meetings; this can be impactful emotional support.

Looking for another book?

Explore our award-winning
books from global business
experts in Human Resources,
Learning and Development

Scan the code to browse

www.koganpage.com/hr-learning-
development